A Little *More* Consideration

RICHARD EHRLICH

AuthorHouse™
1663 Liberty Drive
Bloomington, IN 47403
www.authorhouse.com
Phone: 833-262-8899

This book is printed on acid-free paper.

ISBN: 978-1-6655-2557-2 (sc)
ISBN: 978-1-6655-2558-9 (e)

Print information available on the last page.

Published by AuthorHouse 07/28/2021

authorHOUSE®

For my parents,
Manny and Joyce Ehrlich

for my wife,
Liza

and for my sons,
Jacob and Adam

Contents

Preface

Over the years, I remember my mom telling me more than once "Even the President of the United States uses toilet paper." She said this when she thought I might be doubting myself, when I was facing some challenge that made me hesitate, made me wonder whether I could measure up. She was reminding me that I could play ball with even the smartest and most accomplished of people.

Writing teachers always tell their students "Write about what you know." How could they write about anything else? My writing comes from my life … from my family and friends, from my pain and joy, from my memories and food and movies and dreams. Part of me is always writing for myself and part of me is always writing for "an audience." I'm repeatedly telling my students that everything I'm teaching them I'm also teaching myself. The life lessons we glean from literature – or from anywhere else for that matter – aren't lessons you just learn once and are done; they're lessons to be learned over and over again until they become bone-deep enough to be part of you.

Although these little snapshots of writing are about *my* life, I trust that the messages I'm attempting to give myself are messages you can hear too. Come close, lean over my shoulder and read with me. I'm trying to elevate myself in any way I know how. It's not rocket science, but it's important stuff. Even the President of the United States uses toilet paper.

Ricky Ehrlich
May 2021

Whether I shall turn out to be the hero of my own life, or whether that station will be held by anybody else, these pages must show.

These are the opening words to *David Copperfield*, by Charles Dickens. I like the way they sound here, at the start of my own little book.

Eggs Grandma

She was heavy-set and old, as far back as I can remember. Her face and hands were wrinkled and soft, but strong – something like the ribbed exterior of a bulldog. Thinking back on her now, some three years after her death, takes me to a little shtetl in Poland, to Ellis Island, to the Lower East Side of New York, to Brooklyn in the 1930's. Her eldest daughter once described what she was like as a young woman – that she was so vibrant, so energetic, so downright powerful, that, when she walked, the *ground* actually shook! Even now, I'm still not so sure Aunt Helen was speaking figuratively. Because there's always something remains of youth, of anything we truly were, no matter how far away from it we get.

I remember Grandma cooking and baking at holiday time. We'd all go over there on a Sunday, and she'd be handing out plates of latkes with applesauce, or *ahnsitinkin*. Maybe the last time I was ever over there with her, she made me something … what was it? I wish I could remember. It was at that last place she lived – sort of an older folks apartment building with rails all over the place, benches, and wheel chair ramps. But it wasn't as bad as that sounds. It was in Brooklyn somewhere, not far from where she lived most of her life.

Anyway, it was during the day, and I was keeping her company for a couple hours while dad was seeing one of his clients in the area. I remember, before we went up, dad sent me over to the grocery store on the corner for some bread and milk. I'm not sure, but I'd like to think that what Grandma made me that day was *ahnsitinkin* – loosely scrambled eggs. I'd like to think that because I'm certain she made it for me sometime or other, and I know the entire family has had it, and still does.

It's a very personal kind of dish/memory for me because of the name – *ahnsitinkin*. I mean, I could just say "loosely scrambled eggs," but that's not all they were. There was something *Yiddish* in the eggs, in their preparation, their smell, their taste. The eggs were eyes looking back a hundred years to a time and place when Grandma was herself a grandchild eating *ahnsitinkin*.

The ways of the old world will never be completely dispensed with, anymore than Grandma's wrinkles could completely stop the ground from shaking when she walked. However distant and unapproachable that old world is for me, I still yearn for it; it's still a part of me. Eggs probably smelled the same then as now. Hunger, love, a holiday with grandchildren, and a Grandma cooking and baking, handing out plates to the *kinder* – all the same, all very much the same. And years from now, still, someone will enjoy a plate of *ahnsitinkin*, and taste his family.

Salad For Two: A Mexican Love Story

(Inspired by the film, *When Harry Met Sally*)

Alan and Sheryl were from different worlds, but they both lived in New York. Probably the single major difference between them was that Alan was a man and Sheryl was a woman. This story is not altogether a comedy: it's funny the way real life is funny; it's sad the way real life is sad. But I think it's going to be a basically happy story. After all, in the end, Alan and Sheryl get married and live happily never after. Freudian slip? No; I just want to keep you guessing.

But when I say this is not altogether a comedy, what I mean is, isn't it true about there being a very significant difference a man and a woman? And I'm not talking penis/vagina here, though somewhere along the line I'm sure that has something to do with it. I'm talking years and years of TV and movies and books and relatives and friends and strangers and dreams giving us all kinds of ideas about what a man is and what a woman is. And then we go through all this stuff and embrace what seems to make sense. But the roles of men and women have become so loaded with history, with herstory, it's like trying to learn what driving through Kansas is like while sailing out in Amagansett; things have become a bit more complicated, a bit more nuanced, since the days of Adam and Eve. We can never have the clean slate they had; we start with all sorts of markings that both guide and perplex us. But let's get back to Alan and Sheryl.

In the beginning, they drove each other crazy. One thing in particular he could never understand was that she always read the last page of a book first. This simple fact, in one fell swoop, put to rout everything he believed about order, aesthetics, and the process by which we arrive at meaning. It reminded him of that joke from *The Honeymooners* when Alice didn't laugh at Ralph's joke about the "knight out on a horse." It wasn't that Alice had no sense of humor; hers was simply different from his. The same with Alan and Sheryl: they both had order in their lives; they both somehow arrived at meaning. It would take some time, though, before they could drive their separate meanings without crashing into each other.

They had met in a health-food store on Church Avenue in Brooklyn. His girlfriend had left him four months earlier because he wasn't materialistic enough for her. She had left her boyfriend seven months earlier because, well, it just wasn't right … Doctor Frankenstein tried to combine different parts of different people and look what he came up with. It just doesn't work that way. Everybody is a package deal; you pays your price and you takes your pick.

Anyway, he was looking for the *Gone Nuts* granola and she was looking for some lard-free refried beans. She accidentally knocked down a package of sesame rice cakes and, when they both bent down for it, they knocked heads. A light knock, it wasn't. She just got a little bump, but he was out cold until they brought him back by spritzing him with some Perrier that was conveniently shelved in the same aisle. The first thing he said to her when he came to was, "Are you OK?" Everyone laughed except for Sheryl. She liked his unselfish concern for her and decided to invite him over for lunch. He accepted, provided she'd let him make the salad. They were to have Mexican.

They never did have Mexican that day. The plan had been for Alan to follow Sheryl over to Park Slope where she had an amazing rent-controlled deal going for four years then on an upstairs studio. But, as they were cutting through the Park, her car died, forever. It was towed to her mechanic, Mike, who said it would cost more to fix than it was worth. Sheryl knew Mike a long time and everything he'd ever said about the car had always proven true. So they had Italian on Seventh Avenue, shared a bottle of wine, and agreed to meet the next night for a rain check on the Mexican. They ended up not having Mexican the next night either.

What happened this time was really extraordinary. I mean this is probably the only really unbelievable part of the story. But, I swear, it happened just the way I'm going to tell you: Sheryl had asked Alan to come over around seven and they'd have dinner and maybe rent a video. At 6:22, Sheryl was just finishing the last page of *The Grapes of Wrath* for the first time; she hadn't yet read any other page of the book at that point. If Alan had known this, he probably would never have come for dinner. But he didn't know back then about the way Sheryl started books, and so he was really looking forward to this health-minded young woman and he sharing a dinner of Mexican food and maybe renting a video.

At that same 6:22, Alan was just getting into his car near the intersection of Queens Boulevard and 71st Road when he was told, at gunpoint, to hand over his keys and get into the back seat. Three young hoods, all armed, drove him to a deserted park in Staten Island and left him there. The leader of the gang gave him a quarter and told him there was a pay phone a few blocks east. He apologized for stealing the car, but felt sure Alan would understand. As they drove off in his car, Alan tried to understand. But it was like trying to understand why Sheryl read the last page of *The Grapes of Wrath* before reading any other page. Life could be confusing sometimes.

On the way to the phone, Alan imagined himself a character in a film: he has just been arrested and he's allowed one phone call. "Those guys always call their mothers or their girlfriends or their former cellmates," he said to himself. Alan's mother was in Florida at the time, he didn't have a girlfriend, and he'd never had a cellmate. He was reluctant to use his only quarter to postpone his date with Sheryl, but then he realized that she was probably the only one who would be willing to drive over to Staten Island for something other than visiting a cemetery or conferring with an accountant. So he called her. She knew he couldn't possibly be making all this up, and agreed to pick him up at a nearby diner. She had rented a Nissan Sentra first thing that morning.

By the time Alan and Sheryl sat down to their second meal together, it was around eight o'clock. They considered driving back to Brooklyn for the Mexican food, but Sheryl said she'd put it all away already, figuring there must be some cosmic force at work that did not want her, Alan and Mexican food in the same room together at the same time. In any case, they were both very hungry and decided to have grilled cheese sandwiches and fries right there in the Staten Island diner. They ate and talked until ten, then drove over the bridge into Brooklyn.

Sometime between eleven that night and eight the next morning, Alan and Sheryl made love for the first time. It happened as naturally as the first time they had bumped heads going for the rice cakes, except that, this time, it was *Sheryl* who needed reviving. The first thing she said when she came to was: "That's the first time I've ever done it with a man on the very night his car was stolen." Alan *tried* to interpret this remark in light of what little he remembered from that Intro Psych course he'd taken at Oneonta – wasn't there supposed to be some kind of connection between cars and sexual identity? But he couldn't remember enough of what he'd learned to make any sense of what Sheryl had said and was beginning to realize that some of her thinking would forever be inscrutable to him.

During that first year of their friendship, before love replaced confusion as their primary shared emotion, Alan and Sheryl could often be seen scratching their heads, with bewildered looks on their faces. But now they're very happy together. Sheryl liked the Sentra so much, she went out and bought one the very next week. Alan eventually moved in with her and sold his car, the one that had been stolen that first night he and Sheryl had ever made love. The three young hoods had totaled it, perhaps at the very moment the new lovers were climaxing. It never rode the same after that, though the body-shop guys had made it look brand-new.

Alan and Sheryl were never the same either. And every year, on the anniversary of their first meeting at the health-food store, they make a point of having Mexican food at home. She makes the salad.

The Fifth Period Dream

for my students

It's Saturday morning, maybe even past noon; don't look at the clock much on weekends. I'm in the den with the magazine section from tomorrow's Times — one of the advantages of home delivery. The baby's napping, my wife's out for a walk, the sun is streaming in through gaps in the glass-door curtains. This week's cover story is all about how schools alone cannot save our inner cities. I read a couple pages and start drifting off myself. One minute I'm reading about the crumbling infrastructure of New York City schools; the next, I'm in a dream somewhere, numbers on a door, maybe, can't quite make them out. Wait a second … they're coming into focus now … it's my fifth-period classroom: 452. I open the door and see one of my students is already inside, arranging the chairs into our circle. He hands me his composition. I help to complete the circle by moving one last chair into place and sitting in it. I hesitate starting to read, knowing the late bell is about to ring, not wanting to be interrupted. I start reading anyway. Later on, in my waking life, my wife told me I'd been smiling in my sleep. Here's what I'd been reading, what that kid wrote, made me smile:

Fifth Period

In the beginning, we were all kinda feeling each other out. A few of us had heard good things about this guy Ehrlich who taught *Creative Writing*, but you never could tell. Back in ninth grade, a friend of mine swore by some teacher and so I'd signed up for the class. The guy turned out to be a real loser. My buddy had not intentionally led me astray; for him, the teacher was aces. I guess what it comes down to is that some people simply like vanilla and some like chocolate. There's no definitive right and wrong with these things, just different tastes.

So I took a chance on Ehrlich. I figured, how bad could he be? I kinda liked writing, and how much could they expect from a senior anyway? I mean, didn't some special rights come along with the title or was that just a little more self-deception we'd invented to ease the stress before college? I still don't know the answer to that one. But the thing that clinched it for me was the talk going around the grapevine about all those college profs: they could really dish it out when it came to writing, I'd heard tell, and they were merciless with that damn red pen. I'm sure each of us had his own private reason for taking the class, it being an elective and all, but fear of that red pen was definitely mine.

The teacher seemed to be pretty cool. I remember thinking he was a little uptight in the beginning, just like the rest of us, and that seemed honest, in a way. I mean, we were all in this new little boat together and none of us wanted to rock it too much; none of us knew how much of ourselves it was safe to reveal. The ironic thing is that, later on, after this Emerson dude we'd been reading had managed to open us up a little bit, we realized that the parts we were most afraid to reveal were the very parts that most made us who we were. Hell, I don't think any of us even realized we'd been hiding anything! Sometimes you do something the same way, for so long, you start to believe there's no other way of doing it. But the reading and the writing and the talking were doing their work, were starting to peel off, layer by layer, the mask we'd been wearing, the old paint hiding our true patina.

This nature guy, Thoreau, helped too. He was always going off on some Indian philosophy tangent (the Indian from India, not from here), real spiritual stuff. There was this quote I remember – I'm not even sure it was from Thoreau – but it was definitely his style, right up his alley. It went something like this: *The snake must shed its own skin.*

Somehow, it helped me to hear words like these. We were the snakes, all of us beautiful, living, growing creatures. And it was true; no good could come from rushing our evolution as human beings, as students, as adults, as anything! We, too, were part of nature, and there was a natural progression to our growth that took time, and certainly could not be forced. Vonnegut knew this and tried to teach it to us as Billy Pilgrim, hopping around time to avoid the stupidity of war and all the other atrocities perpetrated by humans who hadn't yet learned the lesson. Gerry tried to teach it to Peter on a park bench in *The Zoo Story*, but Peter was already too far gone to learn a new way and paid for it dearly. The old man in the sea, Santiago, taught it to Manolin and Manolin could not do enough for him in return. He wished to serve the old man in any way he could. He understood that the Tao, the Way of Nature Santiago had taught him, was invaluable and would guide him forever.

And now we were learning it together, fifth period. We were teaching it to each other every day. Ehrlich didn't have all the answers and didn't pretend to. But he had some good questions. And that made us comfortable with *our* good questions. And that was all we needed. I'll remember our circle a long time.

Winter Story in a Hot Room

It's nice to step out of the biting winds of December and step into a steam room. A few days ago, I did just that -- armed with a little bottle of eucalyptus oil. Just a few drops on the bench in the corner fills the whole room with a deliciously scented steam that opens up your nasal passages better than any pill.

But just as I was making my way over to that corner bench, I saw some guy in the act of pouring just ahead of me. "You get that from the health food store?" I asked him. "Nah, this is from a Russian place in Brighton Beach; they make it themselves and it's even more powerful." We started talking as the steam thickened and spread. My first few words to him were all the drops we needed. The conversation deepened and entered our pores, loosened the tight places in us that kept us separate, kept us strangers.

Christmas trees and Chanukah menorahs were coming to life in the cold outside. Behind closed doors, families insulated themselves, locked out the world, hardened the boundaries. But here, at least for a few minutes, all that melted away. A few drops, a few words, were all we needed. Then the magic happened and spread. And we were transformed.

Box Marked "Kosher for Passover"

There's a big box in our laundry room where, for eighteen years, I've been throwing all kinds of excess hardware I think I might need some day. Usually, the stuff stays in there forever. But today was an exception; today, Adam woke up singing.

Maybe he was *kvelling* over his recently acquired big-boy bed. Or maybe he had had a particularly pleasant dream. Perhaps it is simply innate, a predisposition with some kids, to wake up that happy. Whatever it was, our house woke up this morning to his angelic little voice, singing.

I cuddled with him and Liza for a while, then raced over to Great Neck to join my buddies for a few pre-Seder laps; always a good idea to get some exercise in before a family Seder. I had promised mom I'd make the charoset again this year, and figured I'd be at her house around nine. But then she called to say they needed me to stop at Dunkin Donuts. I haven't forgotten about that big box in the laundry room.

By the time I got to mom's kitchen, the old wooden chopping bowl was already in use: dad was making his famous creamy egg salad with onions. I listened, enjoying the sound of his chopping, scraping, chopping; there was a rhythm to it, a kind of music. Soon enough, it was my turn. I started with apples and walnuts, then mixed in some wine and grape juice, some nutmeg and cinnamon, and some honey. Mom thought it looked too walnutty, so I invited her to taste it. Perfect!

Is there anything else you need, mom?

Yes. Tell me what goes where on the Seder plate.

OK.

We started filling the little depressions. I have always loved the brass Hebrew letters bordering this particular plate. It's been in the family longer than any of the others and there are memories attached; there are memories. When we were done, I picked it up and was headed to the dining room table when I noticed one of the handles was loose. Mom said there should be a screwdriver in the little drawer opposite the Fridge. The screw turned and turned, but wouldn't tighten. It was at that moment that I discovered the missing nut.

So now you know where I'm going with this. But do you know what it feels like to truly believe that not one iota of energy was wasted during those long eighteen years, that every single piece of junk I threw into that laundry room box was necessary, was validated this day. Do you know what it feels like to wake up singing?

Israel

Just weeks before we were to depart for our first family trip to Israel, three yeshiva students were kidnapped and murdered. Then, in apparent retaliation, Jewish extremists burned a Palestinian boy to death. Hamas began firing rockets into Israel and it was becoming more and more likely that the Israeli Army would have to enter Gaza. My wife and I seriously considered calling the airline and canceling our flight. Fortunately, several phone calls to friends and family convinced us to forge ahead with our plans. This was nothing new in Israel, they reminded us. Even in the years prior to the State's founding in 1948, Arabs had been attempting to "drive us into the sea." And yet we continue to not only exist, but to thrive. We understood that it would be no more dangerous to travel through southern Israel at this time than it would be to travel through downtown Manhattan. We made our decision and left for the airport.

Although my two sons were more interested in Jerusalem's newest skateboarding park than in the ancient Wailing Wall, I know that seeds were planted in them during this trip that are certain to blossom in their future. As parents, we want our children to embrace our values, but by pushing too much, we may be delaying their learning. The more we say, "keep your hand out of the cookie jar," the more they reach for it. Perhaps it's sometimes true that less is more. Now that I think about it, I did not really embrace my own Judaism until I was a freshman in college, far away from the admonishing voices of my parents.

So we toured the Holy Land both as Jewish pilgrims and as ordinary Americans. We gave our sons small doses of their heritage each day, but made sure they also got whatever food their teenage souls required. We saw the colorful mosaic floor of the Bet Alpha synagogue, but we also saw the colorful candy stall of the Carmel Market. And even when we weren't making any conscious effort to instill a sense of their ancestry within them, I'm sure they couldn't help but feel something special in a place where the Prime Minister, the shopkeeper, the police officer and the garbage man were all Jewish.

Jerusalem was our first stop. The highlight for me was walking through the Jewish Quarter of the Old City just after dark one night. As we took the steps and narrow streets that all seemed to wend their way toward the *Kotel*, the Western Wall, we felt as though we were traveling back in time. The ancient look of the architecture, coupled with the unchanging attire of the people who lived there, enabled you to imagine you were back in another century, way back before the pull of modernity had lured us away from our roots. I felt comfortable among these people. I admired them for their commitment, for their undeviating adherence to a way of life bequeathed to them by their parents, by history, by God.

Next, we traveled toward Afula and Bet Shean. It was especially wonderful to visit the kibbutz where I had worked so many years ago, when I myself was a teenager. Kibbutz Nir-David is situated just downstream of *Gan Hashlosha*, a beautiful national park built around the unique freshwater spring that feeds the *Assi*. Here in the United States, this tiny river would hardly be noticed; but in the semi-desert climate of Israel, this oasis is a magnet for hundreds of people who come to picnic and swim every day of the year. Because it is fed from subterranean aquifers, the water remains the same temperature regardless of the weather. On an especially hot day, it cools you off; during the winter, when it can get a bit chilly there at the base of the Gilboa Mountains, it keeps you warm. We had a restful four days there after the relative tumult of Jerusalem.

Finally, we headed for Tel Aviv. We didn't want to scare the kids with too many details about "the situation," but when sirens started going off, we explained that, although Israel's "Iron Dome" defense system successfully blew up enemy rockets high in the sky, broken fragments of those rockets falling to earth still posed a threat and that's why people had to run for cover. Except for two or three such moments when we were outside and vulnerable, our trip was almost completely unaffected by all the fighting.

We swam in the glorious Mediterranean every day and ate sumptuous, exotic foods every night. I noticed an unusual stop sign at one intersection, so I pulled over to take a picture. In the center of the red hexagon was a hand held up signaling, "stop." What was unusual was that the hand was wrapped in tefillin. Simultaneously, the motorist was commanded to stop his car and reminded to don his phylacteries.

What a marvelous country! Everywhere you go, the mundane is wedded to the sacred, the modern is inextricably bound up with the ancient. I had brought along my father's old siddur and made sure to read a particular prayer from it early one morning. As I recited the Hebrew words thanking God for his myriad creations, I happened to smell something very familiar – grass that had been baking all afternoon in the desert sun.

I remembered that smell from my first trip here, thirty-eight years before, when that precise scent wafted its way up to me on the second floor of my *ulpan*, the pigeons cooing beneath the rafters. I'm sure someone smelled the same distinct aroma in these sacred and cherished environs the year my father was born, in 1930, and two years before that, when my mother took her first breath. It is an intoxicating smell, and it probably helped draw my ancestors ever closer as they approached their Promised Land during those biblical days long and long ago. I imagine that, in the moment that they actually set foot in *Eretz Yisrael*, it must have smelled like heaven.

The Wedding of Shira and Akiva

It was an ordinary Monday night in the surrounding world: traffic backed up on the Throgs Neck Bridge, kids played basketball, lovers shared a meal at a favorite restaurant. But at Marina del Ray in the Bronx, my Uncle's grandson was getting married. Uncle Natie is ninety-one now and has twenty-one grandchildren. Akiva is one of them. As I sat watching the relatives and friends of the bride and groom make their way down the aisle, I saw the history of my life and that of my family passing before me. I saw my roots – fresh and alive and strong. Although my branch of the family did not retain the strictly Orthodox path of my forbears, I still feel a deep kinship with these people, even a tinge of yearning to return to this, to something very precious I lost along the years.

We stood watching as the parents of the groom accompanied him to the *chuppah,* the wedding canopy that is a symbol of God's protection. There, wearing a special robe of sanctity, he waited for his bride. Her parents brought her most of the way to the *chuppah.* Then the groom descended to walk with her the rest of the way. The older trees had bourne their fruit. The young birds were leaving the nest to build a new life together. The new couple had chosen music from the secular world but with words rewritten to suit the occasion, the Hebrew echoing through the hall like mellifluous prayer.

A little earlier, the bride had sat among her maids as her groom approached to lift her veil – an ancient custom established to ensure the man was marrying the right woman. In biblical times, Jacob had been tricked into marrying Leah instead of Rachel; their father had thought it improper that the younger daughter should wed before the elder and so had perpetuated this deception. But today it has evolved into a very beautiful and very public display of the couple's love and commitment to each other. There is an intimacy in these proceedings that can hardly be known to a secular world in which anything goes and little is hidden. We have all heard the expression *less is more,* but it is perhaps nowhere better exemplified than in the modesty, decorum and restraint with which the groom gently lifts his bride's veil and exchanges a few private whispers with her. All around them, a storm of singing and dancing whirls. Within the eye of that storm, the soon-to-be newlyweds share a moment quietly their own, their faces beaming in expectation of the coming nuptials and of a long and happy life together.

The celebration is quiet now. We are back in the ceremony and everyone has arrived. The bride circles her groom seven times, yet another custom passed down through the centuries to purify, to elevate, to sanctify the couple for marriage and for procreation. In the Jewish tradition, married couples – in fact, all of us – are partners with God in the act of creation. Eight days after the birth of a male child, the circumcision is done to complete the work that God has begun. Creation is incomplete without the hand of man. God and man are partners in the world, and the work of repairing the world cannot be done without the ongoing participation of both partners. The extent to which one embraces this perspective certainly informs the manner in which one lives.

Now the seven blessing are made, each one tying the specific marriage here before us today to the larger context of Jewish history, each one progressively deepening their spiritual connection to each other, to their community, and to God. Uncle Natie chants the last of the seven. His voice, though somewhat choked with emotion and softened by age, is still clear and strong, echoing through the large chamber. I glance around me and see faces mostly in rapture, mostly riveted to the sights and sounds emanating from the *chuppah*. But right behind me I'm surprised to see some youngsters busy on their cell phones! Rather than feeling disappointment or anger, I realize that these religious Jews are still part of the secular world; they have simply put up boundaries for themselves, observed the boundaries established by their parents – and those parents observed the boundaries of *their* parents, back through the tide of times. Some will argue that they have cut themselves off from so much, that they are sheltered and cannot possibly see the real world. I would argue that we, each of us, choose what world we make real, what world we live in; and it is primarily in this choosing that the quality of our lives is found.

The prayers come to an end and now the groom, recalling the destruction of the Temple in Jerusalem, smashes the glass. Those same youngsters who had been on their cell phones a few moments earlier now sing louder and dance harder than anyone in the hall. They accompany the bride and groom back down the aisle in a frenzy of joy and celebration. I stand a little bit outside the vortex, not quite a participant, but certainly no stranger to this emotion, this ecstasy. The young groom, after all, is my cousin's son. His grandfather is my uncle. His last name is Ehrlich. But the kinship I most deeply feel in those incomparable moments immediately after his wedding is not a result of the DNA we share in our blood; it is a result of the DNA we share in our heritage. Even if we were not related, I would still feel the magic in this ceremony, in this religion, a magic that binds me to all Jews in all places. I sip nothing but sweetness from this cup. I must immediately say a blessing over this wine: May God grant that I retain this wonderful feeling. May He bless Shira and Akiva with many years of love and health and peace.

May I more fully embrace the perspective that I am partners with God in repairing myself so that I can help in repairing the world.

In Pursuit of Magic

Took a walk in the woods today. It was my first hike as a sixty-year-old and I thought back over all the years I have traversed these particular trails. There are always lessons to learn out in the woods – even on paths you've trod many times before – messages waiting for us to walk by and pick up like so many dropped leaves. Even just last year, I wouldn't have read these particular leaves as I did today. All of intervening Time had colored them for me, made them more noticeable, more blatant. The day had started promising – all sunshine and blue sky – but clouds rolled in thick almost as soon as I got home; two teenagers will do that to you sometimes. Still, I'm blessed. I need to take whatever comes as my fair share and move on. I carry the sunshine of the morning with me into the darkest night. How else could I bear the wait until tomorrow's light?

I had this entire week off from school (Passover) but there were so many things we needed to do that the only free day for me looked like Thursday. I got to bed a little earlier Wednesday and Snickers and I were on the road by six-thirty. Snickers is our almost-three-year-old mix of Rhodesian Ridgeback and Black Mouth Cur. As I drove, I figured Bear Mountain State Park was only an hour and a half away; if we got there by eight and hiked until at least eleven, I'd satisfy my little preference for the total hiking time to exceed the total driving time.

The GPS was saying something about "battery low," but I had gone to this place a hundred times over the years and didn't really need it anyway. If we rely too much upon these things we don't really need, they can actually impede rather than aid our progress. We arrived at that unmarked little parking spot off Perkins Drive someone gifted me thirty years ago just a couple minutes before eight.

I let Snickers roam around on his own while tightening my boots and getting our gear ready. There wasn't much: just some food and water, some treats, the camera, the leash and the cell phone. The phone turned out to be useless because I had neglected to move my reading glasses from the trunk into the backpack and so couldn't see the damn thing well enough to use it. But, again, as I say, unless I was somehow about to get my first compound fracture in a lifetime of hiking, there was no need for it. I'm trying to see the glass as half-full. Someone told me we are blessed to the precise degree that we *think* we are blessed. Of course, nobody gets through life without pain and disappointment; but it's all a question of how you hold your head, as Kesey's Joe-Ben sagely said.

The Appalachian Trail comes up quickly after leaving the parking area and we decided to head south this time. The sun was out full blast now and hardly any wind, but it was still pretty chilly. Soon, though, as we continued to climb, I'd probably be peeling off a layer or two. The air smelled fresh. The birds made music. It took only fifteen minutes to get back into my woods state of mind. Yoga-grade belly breaths came and went easier now, the stress of the recent drive and all the other burdens of life, large and small, melted away, leaving the kind of bone-deep contentment that cannot be grabbed or purchased, and certainly not forced.

I thought of that line Thoreau once wrote about hunters and fishermen having an advantage over other people because their occupations detain them in Nature for such long stretches of time. I always liked the word *detain* in that line because of its subtle irony, its connotation leaning toward the negative. But, really, those hunters and fishermen made a choice: they detained *themselves* in Nature. And so whatever ends up happening in our chosen pursuits is a result of our own intention and therefore something for which we can take credit. Take this idea too far, you're an arrogant person; but take it just far enough, maybe also balance it with a little humility, and you're in business.

I walked on, looking ahead every few steps for the white rectangle of paint that marked the trail. Snickers, the woods heaven for him too, was exploring the terrain, waiting for me only if a sharp turn prevented his sensing me way behind, following. We stopped at a high point overlooking the Hudson and had some lunch. I took a few pictures and stretched out on a little outcropping of smooth rock. Afterwards, we continued south, but the trail soon started getting close enough for us to hear the drone of traffic on the Palisades Parkway, so we turned around and headed back. The car's clock told me I hadn't gotten my full three hours' minimum, so we headed back out on a different trail for another forty minutes or so.

I was back in Long Beach in time for Captain Soot, the chimney guy who had promised to come over and adjust our new flue. The removed-from-Nature chores and routines started swooshing back at me from all sides. But that was not necessarily a bad thing. I knew I'd be back in the woods before long, get my batteries recharged. There's always a yin and a yang in life, something we could term *work* and something we could term *play*. The trick is to keep them in balance, to be especially careful with our choices, our intentions.

That night, reclining on my easy chair in the living room, a small quilt over my legs, my wife nearby on the couch, the lights low and a good movie on the tube, I thought back to something my father once said: the more you chase after respect, the more it eludes you. About halfway through the film, I felt a gentle pressure on my shoulder. It was the hand of my first-born, Jacob, leaning down to hug me and kiss me goodnight. I guess my dad was right: sometimes we need to be still, to give up pursuit, so the magic has a chance to find us.

Mom's Memories

December 26, 2010. Just spoke with mom on the phone. It's Sunday, early afternoon. During our conversation, the idea came to me of asking her to reach back for a memory every time I call her this winter. She's living with her sister Essie down in Florida for a few months and it's not easy for either of them. But she enjoys connecting with me for a few minutes every day and so I figured this would be a good way to record some information, some memories. Since Dad died, I have become a little more conscious of how limited our time is, how precious our loved ones – especially mom. We don't have forever with these people in our lives, but we often behave as though we do. I hang on mom's every word now as I should have hung on Dad's. But we can only do what we're capable of doing at any point in time. What follows are some of mom's memories that I've picked up and pieced together over the last few years:

The first place we lived as a married couple was 308 Sterling Street, on the corner of Nostrand Avenue. We had been working upstate as waiter and waitress for a few months, either at *The Browns* or *The Pines*, and renting an attic apartment in South Fallsburgh. Then my sister Essie bought the apartment where she still lives today and we were able to move into her old place on Sterling Street. It was a six-story building and we were on the second floor. I never used the elevator unless I was pushing a carriage.

Daddy started working at a factory called *Peerless Plastic* on West Street in Manhattan, then switched to a better position with *Singer,* where his brother Heshy was already working. Out on a repair stop one day somewhere on Ocean Parkway, he told the woman who owned the machine that it was now fixed and that there would be no charge; the needle had simply been in backwards. The woman, a Mrs. Ben Maksik, told him that a doctor who helps a patient always gets paid and he was a doctor of sewing machines. When Daddy still refused payment, the woman said he should at least let her do something for him; her husband owned a nightclub in Brooklyn and she could definitely get him a job as a busboy. She gave Daddy the phone number and told him to ask for Vinnie or Angie. Daddy made the call, and was immediately hired as a busboy. Shortly thereafter, he was promoted to waiter and then captain. He was anything but lazy.

After a year or two of selling sewing machines by day and seating people at *Ben Maksik's Town and Country* by night, he got a good tip from his best friend, Alan Katz, who had just recently left *The Herald Tribune.* Alan knew that his former manager was looking to hire someone, so he gave Daddy the guy's name and number. At the interview, the chemistry between them wasn't very good and Daddy didn't get the job. Nevertheless, he kept calling the manager, refusing to give up, but the guy wouldn't give in. Finally, Daddy told him, "Let me work for you without pay for a while, and when you see what kind of a worker I am, you'll change your mind." The manager was so impressed with Daddy's tenacity that he gave him the job. He would work in the city all day and I would meet him at the nightclub with a change of clothes. When he got home at four or five in the morning, I would make coffee, and we would sit in the kitchen, counting the money he had earned that night. He worked at *The Tribune* for a couple or three years, and then the paper suddenly folded. When it did, Daddy immediately found a job as editor of *The Long Island Independent*, a small, local newspaper. He was never without a job.

The Independent didn't pay much, and so Daddy soon acquired a better position as an account executive with *Miller Advertising Agency*. After a while, having garnered many new clients, he was hired by another agency – *Lubell* – where he was making even better money. In fact, he was doing *so* well, that the owners tried to discontinue paying him commissions on one of his most lucrative accounts, *Hemlock Farms*. The manager of this development, a Canadian gentleman named Frank Dembinsky, liked Daddy a lot, and when he heard what was going on at *Lubell*, recommended that Daddy get out of there and open up his own business. Daddy took Frank's advice and never looked back. He took a personal interest in everyone with whom he associated, was always well-liked, and so his clients invariably followed him wherever he went.

He opened his first office in our home at 811 Lowell Street in Woodmere. It was astounding to see the number and complexity of business deals emanating from so tiny a space! But this was because he was so bright and so good at what he did. I remember him sitting in the kitchen, early every morning, compiling a list on a yellow legal pad of things he had to attend to that particular day. There were sometimes as many as twenty-three different items on that list, but, with his memory, he rarely even looked at it. Eventually, he was making enough money to open a new office at 14 West Hawthorne Avenue in Valley Stream. The rest, as they say, is history.

In the eloquent and touching eulogy Uncle Natie gave at Daddy's funeral, he told us that Joseph named his first-born son Menashe because God had allowed Joseph to forget (*nashani*) all his toil and that now, Natie said, "I'm thinking of the toil of a period of eight decades that my brother Menashe, *olav hashalom*, lived."

Ricky … your father didn't have the opportunities that you and your siblings and so many youngsters have today; his parents were from another continent, another century. They didn't have the time or the money to help him very much as he found his way in the world. But he worked hard and gave each of us a far softer life than he ever had, growing up. He was fallible, as we all are, but he was an exceptionally good man. I was extremely lucky to have been by his side for so many years. You remember how he loved everything about President Lincoln? Well, I think it's therefore fitting that my last words about him here should be precisely those that Secretary of War Edwin M. Stanton reportedly uttered at Lincoln's passing … "Now he belongs to the ages."

Of Circles, Presents and Falling Fruit

It was an ordinary morning on the planet. Isaac Cohen was walking his dog, Snickers, along Washington Avenue. After just five minutes, Isaac's life was lightened when Snickers went into his little doody dance. If he doesn't do his dance right away, the traffic starts backing up on Lincoln Avenue and Isaac's ride to work becomes longer and a little harder. It's not a big deal, but many of the moments that add up to our lives aren't big deals. They are little deals that accumulate. And, over time, the sum total of all these deals, the little and the big, is written on our faces, is etched into the way we hold our mouths. The hint of a smile declares to the world that the scales tip in our favor; the hint of a frown, tells the opposite.

We can't fool ourselves or anyone else. An accounting of all the deals we are transacting is forever going on and is, each moment, completely transparent. The happy and generous and loving moments give their weight to our scales, but so do all the others. And the sooner we accept and completely embrace the fact that there can never be any true sweeping of dirt under the rug – the sooner we realize that there is, in fact, no rug; there is only our choice each moment and the irrevocable consequence of that choice, for good or ill – the sooner we truly get that, the sooner we can get on with the business of living a more present-orientated, unashamed and fulfilled life.

Pulling the Prius out onto West Olive Street, Isaac usually tunes into 93.9: NPR news. But today he decides to pop a CD in instead: *Loggins and Messina, Live.* Of course, this completely alters the atmosphere of the morning drive. Although NPR is probably the least toxic of all the news stations, good music is even better. The details of the world always take a back seat to a natural rhythm, to a beat in sync with the planet and the heart behind one's own breastbone.

He stops at the deli and decides to just get oatmeal; last night's pasta and broccoli and baguette go a long way and he's not quite ready for two egg whites on a whole-wheat wrap with spinach and onions. He remembers the Zen master's admonition *Eat when you're hungry; sleep when you're tired* and walks back out to the parking lot, into the rest of his day, with a lighter step, just knowing he made a good little choice. When you think about it, one of those deals we all have going is with food, and what we eat or don't eat definitely adds up over a day, a week, a year, a lifetime. It makes an even bigger difference than what we listen to on our drive to work. There's always an accumulation going on, and the question, really, is what do we wish to accumulate? That doesn't mean over thinking and obsessing every minute of our day; it means evolving very slowly over great chunks of time to a point when our decisions come to us as easily and naturally as fruit dropping from a tree.

Opening his email at school, Isaac reads a near-desperate plea from a student's mother. Apparently, a classmate had taken a picture of her son using his phone in class the day before and the mother is concerned that the photo might be shared, might tarnish her son's reputation. Although there wasn't any exam going on at the time, the image could easily be misconstrued. It's not an emergency, but Isaac thinks of his own two sons, thinks how he would appreciate a teacher going the extra mile right away if either of his two boys faced even the potential for trouble. So, the first chance he's free, he looks up the schedule of the kid who took the picture, pulls him from class and into the hall for a minute and solves the problem; the photo had been sent to only one other student and both of them immediately delete it. The mom is so relieved; she is effusive in her appreciation. Isaac's own mom had always said, "It's nice to be nice." Do we really need any more wisdom than that?

Now, Isaac is back in Long Beach after a long and satisfying day. He had done himself some good and he had done others some good. Isn't that everything? He and Snickers head to the beach to take in another sunset, throw the Frisbee around. They have a nice little routine going: park near Queens Avenue, walk up to the entrance where the boardwalk ends, then head for the dunes. By the time they turn around and head west again, the sun is usually just touching the water, the color spectacular. Instead of rushing home this time, they linger a while… the smells in the air so sweet, the sounds of the surf so soothing. A woman shows up with a beautiful big puppy and the dogs race together in the sand along the shore. They, too, see the orange ball of the sun sinking into the water, their tails wagging with the same fiery energy. Isaac is glad he took his time, that he didn't rush. This gift might not have been given to him otherwise, this present.

It was an ordinary day on the planet; extraordinary things were happening all the time. But you had to slow down enough to notice them. You had to breathe deep, from the belly. You had to keep your head where your feet were. There are a lot of little deals going on every moment of every day and they accumulate; they add up to a very big deal after all.

A few hours pass and stars begin to blanket the night sky. It is time for rest now. Isaac kisses his sons and his wife good night, lines up his clothes for the morning, and checks that the burners on the stove are all off. Just before leaving the living room and heading for bed, he notices Snickers doing his little sleep dance … circling, ensconcing, nestling himself into the deepest, coziest corner of the couch.

There are so many dances in this life and they all somehow follow the same rhythms, the same circular inevitable movements into our essence, our core. Our bodies, our very *lives*, we discover, are microcosms. What is good for the cosmos is good for us. Everything we do is both a little deal and a big deal at one and the same time. But there's no need to fret. We just need to relax, to feel our way into the dance for which we were born, to reach only for those good fruits that our good deeds have attracted to us, ripe and falling before our eyes.

The Wood That Warms Best

A few weeks ago, my son asked me for a ride to his friend's house in St. James. It's a long drive, but Jacob's home on leave from his second year at college and I'm happy to go out of my way for him as long as he does his schoolwork and keeps his nose clean. Also, I figured I'd probably be able to find some good windfall beneath the great trees of the North Shore. I bought myself a Sawzall a couple years ago and have hardly had to buy any firewood since then. Every time I collect some, I'm reminded of what Thoreau wrote in *Walden* – something along the lines of *wood warms you three times: first when you're cutting it, second when you're hauling it, and finally when you're burning it.*

I got two loads of wood out of the St. James deal – one when I dropped him off, one when I picked him up. But the second batch I couldn't manage without his help, so I left it where it was and waited until I had him with me before attempting to get it into the car. I had wedged a huge branch between two trees to break it, but couldn't handle it alone. With four hands, however, it was a piece of cake. We pushed all our weight against the branch, broke it, fit the two pieces in the car (with barely an inch to spare) and were on our way.

There was easily an hour's worth of daylight by the time we got home, so I told Jacob I'd take the dog to the beach first and then we'd deal with the wood; there was rain in the forecast, so I wanted to get it cut and covered before nightfall. Snickers enjoyed his run along the surf and I got home with just enough light to work with Jacob. Having him hold the wood while I made each cut made it so much simpler; it's very awkward for me when I do it alone: the branch is resting on cinder blocks a few inches above the concrete driveway and I have to hold it steady with one foot while gripping the saw tightly with both hands. I always feel a little off balance doing it and I'm lucky if I finish without messing up my back. It was a pleasure working out there with my teenage son those few minutes, the two of us together, the quieting of evening almost palpable whenever the saw stopped, the end-of-the-day light bathing everything in its soft, calming glow.

When we were done, he headed inside to his computer and his phone, away from this momentary disruption in his young routine to help his old dad. Don't get me wrong; I'm not complaining. I'm happy he's willing to help me out when I ask. He's a good kid and I love him. At nineteen, he's not supposed to be thinking the way I do at sixty-one. But everything counts, right? So by including him in my activity, by getting him off-line and tuned into something real for a change – fresh air in his lungs, natural wood in his hands – maybe I'm helping *him* as much as he's helping me. Do all parents think this way or am I just plain bizarre?

I headed into the garage for a tarp. Luckily, I saw one right there in the front; I think I used it last winter to cover one of the air conditioners on the east side of the house. First, I opened it up to see which side would be better to face the sky; I remembered one side had hems that would hold rather than deflect water. Next, I folded it enough to cover the wood without too much left over for the wind to mess with. I then secured it with some paving stones we had lined up along the garbage cans. Initially, I thought I would use only three or four of them; they're pretty heavy and my back doesn't need any more lifting than is absolutely necessary. But I ended up using all six.

I took my time there in the driveway. The sun was already down by then, but enough light still lingered in the west for me to see what I was doing. I pinned the top edge of the tarp against the driveway wall and the bottom edge against the driveway itself. I knew that by being more careful here and now I was making it way more likely that the wood would stay completely dry, no matter how hard the rain or how strong the wind. I kept adjusting the paving stones, kept moving them around to make sure they were equidistant. I kept pulling the tarp taut, knowing that the high winds coming off the ocean could cause a lot of flapping, could loosen the straight line of my roof and allow water to pool instead of run off. I considered the forces at work here, considered more than just the present moment. I thought about tomorrow, next week. In my mind, the present included what the future could bring. I did not rush what I was doing.

Every morning now, when I leave the house and head down the front steps, I see that little roof I constructed out of that tarp and those six stones. I see the previous night's rain beaded on its surface. I think of all the hours that have passed since then, all the rain and snow my little creation has kept off that wood. Sometimes, I'll take a peek underneath to reassure myself that everything's still dry, that all the extra time I took was worth it. I guess a job well done is something like that wood Thoreau wrote about; it warms you (at least) three times: first while you're doing it, second when you've just finished and feel that sweet satisfaction of having completed something of quality, and then again and again and again every time you see it and bathe yourself in the knowledge that your good work keeps on working, that not one iota of the energy you expended had been in vain.

And now my thoughts jump from that little job in the driveway to something big and important, something like the way I see myself and what I'm capable of. That silly little roof I made becomes something really significant, becomes a flashing sign reminding me that the quality of my sleep each night – indeed, my overall self esteem – is forged not just by what I do each day but also by *how* I do what I do each day. When I do my best at every task, even the seemingly insignificant ones, when I get *out* of the habit of looking for short cuts and instead get *into* the habit of making the quality of the job I do more important than the time it takes, the dividends keep paying off. And what I accrue with this way of behaving, with this way of thinking, is far more valuable than money; it's my conception of myself. And when that conception is up where it belongs, I begin to walk around with my head held high, genuinely proud of myself, instead of skulking around. And it's not the arrogant kind of pride. It's the quiet kind, the kind that isn't for any parent or teacher or friend or colleague; it's for me. Over time, not overnight, I develop the kind of self-image that makes anything possible. I am finally able to smile inwardly and deeply as I consider and fully embrace those words I'd heard so many times before but couldn't really believe: *You are the architect of your life.* When I remember this Truth, time is my friend instead of my enemy. I no longer watch the clock; I watch what I'm doing. And instead of keeping myself down by making a half-assed effort at whatever I'm engaged in, I lift myself up, take my time sweet, and begin to feel the warmth of the wood that warms best.

Tikun Olam

Went camping in the Adirondacks with three other men this week. I'll try to put into words some of what we experienced there together, but it ain't going to be easy; what we experienced there was beyond words. What we did together there was, I think, more nearly aligned with and expressible through the imagery of *Kabbalah*, the teachings of ancient Jewish mysticism. According to the *Zohar*, because G-d is infinite, in order to create the physical world, He had to create a "space" within Himself where such a world could exist. To accomplish this, He first created *keylim* (vessels), which He filled with His light. But His light was too intense for the *keylim* and they shattered, the "pieces" scattering into the world, into the space of physicality. Our job in this life is to gather those shards, a process known as *tikkun olam (*repairing the world*)*. Through good deeds, love, generosity, and self-growth, we bring these sparks/shards of holiness back together and repair the world. We reunite the physical with the spiritual. We elevate our brethren and ourselves and reconnect with our Infinite origins.

The beauty of the Adirondacks alone is enough to inspire anyone, enough to help one sense the spiritual core of the earth and of our lives. But when that beauty is coupled with friendship, with laughter, with four guys jumping from rock to rock and moment to moment as though Time had stood still for them, then a new window has been opened and a dimension of Life never before imagined becomes possible, becomes real, is tasted and felt and breathed … breathed deeply.

The time we had on this camping trip truly deserves the word sublime. It was as though our senses had been sharpened to a degree we had never known before. The walks we took were more interesting, the swims were more refreshing, the meals were more nourishing and delicious. There was a symbiosis going on between the spirit of the place and the spirit of our companionship that would have been impossible to believe had we not experienced it for ourselves. But every step along the winding trails, every plunge into the pristine waters, every mouth full of Noon Mark's meals confirmed for us that we were not dreaming, that we had passed a boundary of some kind and would never be the same. Guardian Rock, I know, stands there now, solid and rooted, waiting patiently for the new moon, waiting patiently for our return next year.

We were four guys who had already built up some love and trust before meeting there at the side of that road in Keene Valley, New York at one o'clock on a Thursday afternoon in late August. We already knew each other and liked each other. We already had some good vibes going out into the universe and toward each other. And I guess the sparks of what little fire we already had going between us were fanned by the winds and the waters and the mountains of that magical place into a blaze that lifted us and warmed us to heights and comforts we had never known before. Our love and our reverence for Nature and for each other rejuvenated our bodies and our spirits, opened us, enlightened us. Never shall I forget our two days and nights in those woods. I understand now that what we were doing there was *tikun olam:* by repairing ourselves, we were repairing the world.

Using Ideas As My Maps

That's what each of us is doing every day. Things pop into our heads and we follow them to their predictable destinations. But the problem for me is that I'm often too zoomed in to see the full continent of my present moment. I think that this street, this river, is the entire world and I fail to see the many avenues, the many tributaries just waiting for me to dip an oar and guide my boat into new and unimagined waters. The world is an oyster, but you don't crack it open sitting on a mattress. I've got to get out there and explore, plant my feet on the naked earth and walk great distances, see beyond the contours of what someone else has already navigated and go my own way. At the same time, history is an important teacher. I can and should observe carefully what others have said and done and allow their experiences to inform my ever-expanding itinerary. But their limitations need not become mine. What others have achieved or modeled for me are simply markers saying: *Here are some roads, some paths to travel; perhaps you will find them useful for a time. And, when your life leads you elsewhere, as it surely will, never forget the crucial role those first paths played in providing your earliest and, perhaps, most salutary guidance. Remember them. Remember to have gratitude for them and for the people who put them on your map.*

It's always a question of balance. Sons want freedom from their father's advice, but they're also conflicted about it. They know what the father says is true, but want to discover it for themselves, want to finally feel the independence of manhood. Then again, the father's truth is not exactly the sons' truth and so the father, too, must learn about balance: if he guides too much, he steers his sons away from their true directions; if he doesn't steer at all, he fails to provide those few crucial signposts that might have made all the difference in his boys' journeys.

And then there is Time. Although it is not some tangible place we can point to on our Life Map, it is nevertheless present at every single intersection of latitude and longitude. The past is part of where we are now and the future is too, for all we cannot see it. I remember, way back in my high school days, hanging out with my friends on a Friday or a Saturday night. I'd start heading out the door at around 11:30 or so and someone would yell, "Where the hell you going, Ehrlich? The night is young!" I'd say something like, "I have track practice in the morning" or "I'm going to Temple tomorrow with my dad." They'd all look at me as though I were crazy. What did tomorrow have to do with tonight? They probably thought I was a little strange and they were right. I was.

But my strangeness has served me very well over the years. To this day, if I drink more than one beer or a half-glass of wine, I wake up with a hangover. Gradually, over many years, I found the confidence to ignore more and more of the peer pressure that we all encounter. Which ideas do I follow and which do I ignore? Even today, at sixty-two, there are still those who want me to follow their lead, to be just like them, to join them in their behaviors. But, when I'm smart, when I'm at the top of my game, I'm able to hear that quiet voice that's always whispering to me from deep under my own breastbone. I'm able to listen to that voice, ignore their judgment, and go my own way.

Yesterday, I was sitting quietly in our living room reading when my wife informed me there was a teaching job available at my old high school. She had told me to check online first thing in the morning, but I had forgotten. There's no great emergency for me to work anymore; thirty-two years of teaching enabled me to squirrel away quite a nice nest egg. Quite nice in my book, that is. We'll never be rich as far as money goes, but there are other ways by which wealth can be measured. Still, a little more money than I managed to sock away so far might come in handy one day – especially with two kids and their incessant trips to the frig. So I told her to click the "Yes, I accept" option. My day suddenly shifted from quiet reading to frenetic activity; I had to be in Great Neck by 7:45 and I had nothing ready.

In the end, though, I was glad she had told me about the job. Long-ago interactions with students were still paying dividends. When Emily's mom, a math teacher at the school, learned I'd be her partner for the day, she immediately face-timed her girl up at college. Good vibes accruing since Emily first took her seat in the center row of my tenth-grade English class, four years ago, washed over us now. When I saw Jake in the hall and learned that he had just been hired as a Spanish teacher, he told me, even though it's been over ten years since I was his teacher, that I was largely responsible for his present good fortune. My past, like some kind of magical yeast, was shaping my present, helping it rise, bringing it to fruition. Time was doing its eternal work. I must remember that what I am doing right now is never just about what I am doing right now. It is always about yesterday, too. It is always about tomorrow, too. I simply can't see that part because I haven't arrived there yet. But seeds are being planted every moment. They are growing incrementally, invisibly, like corn in the night, and every one of them will eventually sprout its tiny but definite contribution to the overall Design.

My good buddy Mitch tells me he will keep updating the maps on my GPS, that changes are always happening and you never know when an update might prove to be handy. I need to remember this and apply it to my Life Map. Changes are always happening and you never know when an update might prove to be handy. There are roads ahead of me I could never imagine, not even with the most meticulous planning, and so I must pay attention. I must remain fully alert for new turns, new ideas.

Josh and Michelle are honeymooning in Europe and they made specific plans for the first two nights only; the other thirteen they intentionally left open to adventure. My friends are always teaching me, opening me to new paths, new waters. I must turn off this lazy, robotic cruise control and take back my autonomy, take back this eternal present being offered if I'm awake enough to embrace it. A turn of the wheel, a dip of the oar, and a new horizon immediately beckons. There is still so much road ahead, so much day yet to dawn. The sun is but a morning star.

The title of this writing is from Dylan.
The final sentence is from Thoreau.

36

Golf Ball on a Tombstone

When you've lived over six decades, you begin to think a little differently. Truth is, it's not just those of us who have lived that long; it's everybody. Our thinking is always shifting. Our lives are tiny rafts making their way across a huge, magnificent ocean, our One Great Sea, and every experience is a kind of wave we feel and absorb and remember. Some are big and some are small. Some push us gently in the direction we wish to go, some threaten to drown us. Some are so insignificant that we hardly notice them; but some enter into us, become bone-deep memory, become part of the story we tell ourselves about ourselves. If we're lucky and we stay afloat long enough, the story gets better. If we're *really* lucky, the memories blend into a kind of ballast, a unique and very personal center of gravity that allows us to negotiate the rapids of life with an equanimity we could never have imagined way back in our early days, when we feared them, when we battled them. If I tried to put all my important memories down here now, I wouldn't have any time left to find new ones. So I'll just put down a few – one from each decade – that brushed their colors into my self-portrait, that nudged me, however slightly, into my right direction.

When I was in second grade, there was a playground on the roof of our yeshiva in Brooklyn where we played punchball just about every day. When the ball went over the fence, as it did from time to time, one of us had to scamper down to retrieve it out on Kings Highway. We probably sneaked out to do it; I can't imagine the teachers giving us permission with all those cars and busses flying by. We always got out early on Friday so there'd be plenty of time to prepare for the Sabbath. This one particular Friday, I was on the school bus heading home when the driver abruptly told us to quiet down, that he'd heard a report come over the radio about the President. I couldn't be sure, but I had the feeling that something serious had happened. I ran down our quiet Manhattan Beach sidewalk, opened the front door of our rented apartment, and found my mother hysterically crying in front of the TV; President Kennedy had been killed. I was seven years old and I watched every minute of the funeral on that black and white TV, watched that little boy stand at attention and salute his slain father.

From my second decade, I remember the day in ninth grade that John Ross and I tried out for the JV basketball team. We were the two smallest guys on the court, but, somehow, we had survived the first cut. We were so elated that, when we got out on Seagirt Boulevard for our ride home, we were still jumping and dancing around in delirious celebration. John danced a bit too far out into the street and a small truck suddenly screeched to a stop right in front of him, actually hitting him and knocking him to the ground. He immediately sprang up and brushed himself off as though he were Superman.

Sometime in my third decade, I finally accompanied my friend Dave Neylon to his brother's property in Jamaica, West Indies. This was in 1977. I was twenty-one and had just one year of college under my belt. Dave had been inviting me for years, but one thing or another came up and we never made it happen. This time, though, I was one of five lucky twenty-somethings and one old guitar all piled into someone's mom's car and heading for Florida. We spent New Year's Eve at Billy Crystal's house in Coconut Grove and Dave and I flew to Montego Bay on January second. For two months, we slept in a tent, watered Bill's fruit trees, and enjoyed Rose's Sunday night dinner. I remember, one crisp, blue-sky day, Dave led me to a cliff from which you could jump off into the Caribbean. The jump was around thirty-five feet. It was scary, but we watched several people do it safely and so we psyched each other up for the experience and took off. The jump itself was amazing, but that wasn't all. Right after surfacing, you swam into this spectacular multi-colored cave and climbed up, the tide sloshing the walls around you, into Mr. Joseph's front yard for another jump. The place was known as "Joseph's Cave."

Jamaica was just a small part of two-and-and-a-half years I spent bumming around after that one year of college, trying to figure out what I was going to do with the rest of my life. But I did return to school, completed an M.A. in English, and was working on a second Masters, when, in 1986, on the cusp of my fourth decade, I remember noticing an ad in one of the New York papers reading, "Three Hundred Teachers Needed." I was really tired of sharing a bathroom with three other guys and never having any money. I was thinking maybe it was high time I branched out a bit beyond the confines of the student life. So I went downtown to see about getting a real job. There must have been nine hundred people crammed into this low-ceilinged NYC Board of Education facility. After waiting endlessly on line after line, we finally completed the dreadful application procedure and were told to return on Wednesday. This was a Monday. On my way out, something told me to step into a side office that caught my eye and ask the lady sitting in there, "Is there any way I can expedite this process?" In a very quiet voice, she said something, but I couldn't hear what it was. "Excuse me?" I asked. "Come back tomorrow," she whispered. I walked in the next day to a completely empty hall, handed someone my papers, and was told to take the second door on the right and see Mr. Rufus Thomas. This man immediately stamped one of my papers and gave me subway directions to a place called Wingate High School in Brooklyn. I taught there for the next eleven-and-a-half years.

It was at Wingate that I met the beautiful young lady I would eventually marry. The venue had been arranged, years before, when I had asked my cousin Beverly for permission to be wed at her place, The Castle, when the right girl came along. She gave her blessing immediately. We called her place "The Castle" because its old stone walls and surrounding grounds presented an environment that was nothing less than regal. By the time our chosen month finally arrived – August 1996 – my fifth decade had already begun. I remember Liza and I making sure all the preparations were well underway before taking off on our own, the day before the wedding, in search of natural waters; it is Jewish tradition to immerse oneself in a *mikvah* prior to one's wedding. We thought a wild *mikvah* would be more appropriate than a man-made one, but there was no public access to any of the lakes near Bedford Hills. We had to drive farther than we had intended, but it was totally worth it. We ended up performing our private ritual in the pristine waters of God's Little Acre. It was pouring rain and the swimming hole was freezing, but the spiritual parts of us were now cleansed and ready to be united. Of course, our iced bodies needed loving attention too and so we blasted the heat of the Honda on our way to the motel.

In 2006, in my sixth decade, Super Storm Sandy surged up over Long Beach and brought five feet of water into our basement. The town looked like a war zone with mounds of ruined belongings piled high on every sidewalk waiting to be carted away. Special areas were set up for the collection and safe disposal of toxic materials. But, despite all the gloom, what I remember best of that time is the way our friends took care of us. Judy and Bernie gave us a car so I could get to work in Great Neck and the Soffers invited all of us into their home until our power and water were back to normal. We even managed to attend Sammy Spear's Bar Mitzvah in the city just a few days after the storm.

Waves of experience, waves of memory, each one washing over us, carrying us, moving us, shaping us. It is now 2019 and I am in my seventh decade. It is January twenty-third, my father's birthday. He would have been eighty-nine. My mother asks me to take her to his grave. It is a tradition with us. I tell her I'll pick her up at seven. She is concerned that the cemetery won't be open so early. I tell her not to worry, that by the time we get there, it'll be open. We take the Loop into the Meadowbrook into the Southern State. We get off the Pinelawn exit and follow the long straightaway to Beth Moses. I unintentionally turn into the first entrance instead of the third, but we know how to go that way too, so it's not a problem. We make the last right turn onto Ezra Road. We park the car. We get out. I take mom's arm so she won't trip on the uneven ground. We approach the grave. And then, we see it, right there in front of us: someone left a golf ball on top of the tombstone instead of a rock; Dad was an avid golfer and would have loved the gesture. I have no idea who left the ball there, but for now and forever it is one more memory to mix in with all the others, to think about, to tip the scales of light and darkness, to help me smile as I continue to live, as I continue to remember and remember and remember, as my tiny boat glides down the ages, as I hurtle, with an ever-deepening gratitude, through the channels of our One Great Sea.

For my Big Brother, Bobby

When I was around ten years old or so, my brother Bobby and I were exploring some monkey bars down toward the western end of the boardwalk in Long Beach, our hometown. I think it was wintertime, so the place was pretty desolate; the bars were part of a summer camp called *Sun and Fun,* or something close to that. Usually, a distinct advantage about exploring when one is still a boy is that the adult compunction to walk beside your companion, to compromise your autonomy in the name of social cohesion, has not yet intruded itself upon one's consciousness. Bobby was doing his thing and I was doing mine. I was high up in the bars (I think it was supposed to be a spaceship), Bobby had wandered off somewhere – perhaps to canvass the ever-changing terrain under the boardwalk; to this day, I still have no idea. Anyway, we were both too fully immersed in our own private worlds to feel even the slightest anxiety about any social responsibility. As I said, this was usually an advantage. Not this time.

All of a sudden, I heard and saw three kids, all bigger than me, starting to climb my way and muttering things that made me feel afraid. There certainly had not been many times, if any, at that early point in my life, when I feared for my safety, nor have there been many since then. But I distinctly remember feeling that these guys intended to hurt me. The fear I felt was very different from that which arose from failing a test or getting caught stealing a candy bar. This was an elemental, bone-deep fear that came from the animal part of me, the part that was about life and death and nothing else. I only felt it for a few seconds, but I shall never forget it.

Then, out of nowhere, I heard and saw my big brother jogging toward the base of the bars, yelling something, threatening the three kids. I don't think he was much bigger than they were and we were certainly still outnumbered. I guess it was his sheer presence, the unyielding force of his intention, that scared the kids away.

I'm sixty-two years old now and life has thrown many curve balls my way. A few times, they have even curved enough to make me fear my end was imminent. But, mostly, I have been unafraid and happy. And in some mysterious, but very definite way, I feel certain that Bobby's saving me that day long and long ago is part of the reason.

Omniscient Narrator

Every so often, when I'm in the middle of doing some ordinary thing in my ordinary, every-day life, I'll imagine what the scene I'm living in would look like as part of a movie or a book. I'll momentarily get outside my head and start looking down from some lofty, bird's eye view, start watching the tape playing before my eyes – of my real life right then and there – but with the very substantial difference that now I'm imagining it all as though it's part of a film shoot or a novel: I'm watching the scene as though someone else is filming all this and I'm just one of the actors; I'm thinking the lines a narrator might use to describe all this and I'm just one of the characters.

For example, just yesterday, I was at the beach with Snickers, my beautiful five-and-a-half-year-old Rhodesian Ridgeback/Black Mouth Cur mix. We were doing our usual, ordinary thing: I was throwing his favorite ball and he was sprinting for it, diving onto it and then playfully moving away from me whenever I approached for another throw. My sternest voice convinces him to stop so I can wrench the ball free from the iron grip of his jaws. I make sure to do at least five long throws before even thinking about leaving; this is the one time all day he gets to run full throttle and he loves it. The water was at low tide and the sun was sinking in the west, already coloring the clouds out toward the horizon. Workers at the beach club were doing winter maintenance, repairing or replacing walls and roofs for the coming season. The winds and the waves were more consistent, more prominent, than the sounds of their drills and their hammers and so these human noises were relegated to background; they complemented rather than infringed upon the overall serenity of that secluded place. The dune grass swayed back and forth with the shifting ocean breezes.

As my eyes began to pan along the wooden fencing that had been set up there to conserve the sand, I started listening to the words playing in my head, words a narrator might use to describe the scene:

A bearded man and his dog walk along the beach. The man, call him Jared, carefully inserts an orange ball into the curved end of his throwing stick, making sure it's tightly ensconced so as to ensure a smooth flight. He then runs a bit forward, for momentum, as he concentrates all his energy into his aged, but still relatively muscular right arm. Although encumbered by a down parka and shearling mittens, he still calls to mind a javelin thrower at the finals of the Olympic Games, the crowd holding its collective breath in the split seconds between the release of his missile and the marking of its landing. He watches the dog sprint toward the ball that is now arcing high into the air, now landing, now rolling in the distance. Way beyond the fencing, the dog is almost upon the now motionless ball of prey. Still several feet away, he leaps for it, his front paws, like talons, fully extended and grasping, and then (zoom in/close-up) the sand exploding, spraying out from the epicenter of his violent landing and slide, the ball now invisible, buried deep beneath him.

As Jared jogs toward the dog for another throw, last night's dream returns to him. He had been earnestly talking to some guy out of his remote past, maybe as far back as high school, a very popular guy, the leader of the pack, trying to articulate, to confess, his fervent wish that they finally accept him, that he just once be allowed to step beyond the periphery and be fully embraced as a member of the group. This guy had the power to anoint him, but would he? Jared wonders what brought back the dream, what it meant. Could it have something to do with the friendly banter among old friends he'd overheard in the steam room the day before? Every one of those guys had grown up together, attended the same schools, the same church. They were part of a group he had never been in, a club he could never join.

Now he has wrestled the ball back out of the dog's powerful maw and he must concentrate, must return fully to the present; the Rhodesian Cur is jumping all around him, clawing in blissful desperation to get the toy. Jared fakes one way to get some room, then, once again, runs a bit forward, for momentum, as he concentrates all his energy into his right arm. The ball is in flight now, the dog sprinting, the waves crashing in rhythmic percussion to the workers' drill and hammer. A lone seagull sails over the dunes toward the open sea. The night dream is carried off by the wind, its images and ideas whisked away, like ocean foam scudding along a shoreline. Jared is thrust back into his present, his waking life. He pictures the sands of some great, relentless hourglass measuring time, showing what is lost and what is gained with every passing day. He smiles at the thought that this same glass will be turned over as soon as it's empty, says to himself, with determination, "Next time it does – tomorrow – I must be more conscious, more awake … more grateful."

It was getting late and I started thinking about dinner, the recliners in our living room, and the afghans we'd have across our legs. I pointed the stick toward the parking lot and yelled, "Car!" Snickers immediately complied, tired enough to be satisfied and willing to leave the beach. I got his bowl out of the back seat, poured in a bottle's worth of water, and added a treat broken in four. We pulled out of the lot, made the right onto Beech, and headed for home, the sun an orange ball behind us, both of us looking forward to warmth, to rest, to stillness.

Another good day was ending. Adam came upstairs and said goodnight; a bit later, Liza turned in too. I checked the downstairs and the stove knobs, peed, then headed for bed and some quiet reading. Before long, as expected, my eyes began to close; the book started slipping from my hands. I reached for the lamp, rolled the switch between thumb and index finger until it locked into its distinctive click. In the blackness of the room, I did my little meditation, inwardly pronouncing the Hebrew mantra with every exhale. My breathing gradually slowed and I soon found myself, once again, in the land of dream. In this mysterious realm, I was no longer conscious of much, but was still acutely aware, somehow, that an omniscient Director was still right there with me, was *always* with me – in every scene, the dream life and the waking life – encouraging me, motivating me, forever whispering His one magical word. I can almost see Him smiling as He says it, can almost feel His hand pushing me forward, but gently, as He pronounces it … *"Action!"*

Remembering Dad

My father died on February 23rd, 2010. On the Jewish calendar, which is determined by the earth's relative position to the moon rather than to the sun, he died on the ninth day of *Adar*. This was his mother's *yurtzeit*, Yiddish for "death anniversary." My Uncle Natie, in his beautiful eulogy at the funeral, said it was as though their mother's soul were coming down to welcome his brother into the heavenly spheres. Jewish law and custom demands recognition of a person's death anniversary rather than his birth anniversary because, when a person is born, he has not yet done anything with his life, not yet accomplished anything, and so there is really nothing much to celebrate. When a person dies, however, we can look back on all he has accomplished in the years he was given on this earth, all the little contributions he made toward *tikun olam*, "repairing the world."

My parents returned from their annual trip to Israel on November 16th, a Monday. I picked them up at Kennedy, making sure to bring along the Celene Dion Christmas CD; a couple of the songs on it were so spectacular, I knew my father would love hearing them again. He was most open-minded when it came to music. Ironically, it was my mother, who came from a relatively irreligious family, who would cringe whenever the name "Jesus" was mentioned in a song; my father couldn't have cared less. The beauty of the instrumentation and the vocals dominated his perception and elevated it to a place where the name of one's God or one's religion no longer mattered to him. I guess when someone loves something deeply enough, that love carries him away from his normal prejudices, the parts of him that are ordinary or even small. My father loved music and he was at his best in its environs. Music lifted him to another level.

I'm pretty sure I picked them up in his big Lexus, not my little Honda, and that I stayed behind the wheel for the drive home. He had driven us all so many miles over so many years, it's hard to see him as a passenger; but I can. Some of my most cherished memories of us together were those annual jaunts we took to Albany to renew his NYP plates. I often drove the three-and-a-half hours back home while he napped. It felt especially good to perform that small service for him; he had always done so much for me.

The next morning, Tuesday, Dad went to see his doctor. This was the guy who'd given him the green light to fly months earlier (Dad hadn't been himself for at least a year or so and Mom had insisted he get an exam before they left). At this post-trip check-up, he slipped and fell in the bathroom and was taken to the hospital for a more thorough evaluation. Tests revealed that his kidneys were no longer functioning properly and so toxins were accumulating in his blood; this is probably why he lost his balance at the doctor's.

Except for one day, his birthday, January 23rd, he remained in the hospital, or the rehabilitation center, which wasn't much better, until the day he died. Those final three months were agonizing for him and for all of us. Although his body was steadily deteriorating, he never lost his incredibly sharp mind. This made it even harder for him because he fully recognized the incompetence and stupidity, the Keystone-Cop-like quality of the care he was receiving. There was a different doctor for each part of his anatomy, and their communication with each other was inconsistent and often confused; sometimes it was even contradictory. We understood that he was very sick, but it was very frustrating to witness the circus playing around him while we were all so powerless to intervene.

In the final days, he passed in and out of a coma. I was alone with him at the end. When I thought his breathing had stopped completely, I called the nurse in to check for a pulse and took note of the time. His soul left his body just before sunset on the ninth of *Adar*. Thinking of that day now, nine years later, I can hear, again, Uncle Natie's words at the funeral. I see Grandma descending a beautiful golden ladder. I see her taking Dad's hand, gently, making it easy for him, removing every fear. I see her holding her head high, mouth spread in a smile, proud of her son, as she guides him up the golden rungs to his well-earned place in the Heavenly Spheres.

Living the Dream

Back in 1998, I had a disturbing dream. I was driving along somewhere, but missed a sharp turn and had to back up. Dense foliage made it difficult to see and, although I was going very slowly, I felt the car moving off the road and onto dirt. Suddenly, the back of the car dropped. My first thought was, "Oh shit, I've hit a ditch!" But, inexplicably, nightmarishly, the car continued to fall. The little bit of light at the top quickly disappeared and I felt the oxygen being sucked out of my lungs. I had a moment of deep sadness, realizing my life was ending … and then I woke up.

What miracles our dreams are! What miracles the lives we wake up to! But it's a package deal of good and bad and the sooner we wake up to that fact, the better off we'll be. My sister was going through a divorce then and I had visited her new home for the first time earlier that week. While checking out her yard, I noticed an old wrought-iron table that looked kind of familiar. I soon realized it had belonged to my parents – it was the one with the white frame and glass top that was originally in their Woodmere kitchen, then moved out to the southeast corner of their yard, near the pool.

Both of my parents were still alive back in 1997, when I had this dream about the car falling, when I visited my sister and saw the table in her yard. Life presents beautiful moments and scary moments. There is not always a direct correspondence between what we experience and what we dream. But, if we think about it long and hard enough, we can sometimes discover the origin of a dream in the life. Dreams are fuzzy, mysterious things. Even when we can't pinpoint exactly where one came from, we can still try to understand the message our subconscious is trying to send us.

Seeing the table in my sister's backyard that day, covered with dirt, I remember thinking about the transience of life – in particular, of my *parents'* life. Was this more of a thought or more of a feeling? Seeing the table in this new context, I was struck with the feeling/thought that my parents were getting older, that the things which, for many years, were part of our stable life together were starting to unravel, to decompose. Eventually, I knew, their very bodies would follow.

The nightmare of falling to my death is far more dramatic than a little sadness over the passage of time, but perhaps the two are parts of the same miraculous continuum. Even though all we ever have is time, we can use some of that time to remember. Remembering allows us to multiply time, to expand it. Maybe remembering can even bestow a kind of immortality on the people and things that we hold most dear. By remembering them, the people live again, just as colorful and alive as when they were swimming in the pool. By remembering them, the tables are once again sparkling clean, holding all those mouth-watering dishes at mom and dad's annual Fourth of July party.

You may think it's a stretch to connect this particular dream with this particular life moment, but, as Alice said in *Wonderland*, "Life, what is it but a dream?" Indeed. All we ever have is the present moment. But, when we remember, all the moments we've ever had in our lives are present as well.

Proof

There is a God. How can there not be? I'm sitting here in Great Neck South High School where I substitute teach two or three days a week. The students have their assignment online and so I have some time to sit back and read. In just a few minutes, an Isaac Bashevis Singer story whisks me away to Poland in 1924. I am completely transported to this particular long-ago place and time, to this ramshackle room in which a man and a woman, two fictional characters, are conversing. I am feeling their feelings, hearing the sounds outside their window, smelling the smells of their village. But it is really *Singer's* village, is it not? It is the tiny Polish village he came from, indelibly etched into his memory fifty or sixty years before. Because, at its core, all writing is autobiographical, no matter how well we dress it in fictional clothing. Those same smells, those same feelings, still fresh all these years later! What a miracle to sit here, reading another man's words, and to be so engrossed, so captivated, so suddenly and fully in his long-ago world!

But, of course, it is not Singer's story alone that convinces me. It is everything. It is birdsong in the morning. Is anything else as hopeful, as encouraging? That natural music beckons me to rise and meet the day, reassures me that the long night is over, that the last wisps of mist and darkness will quickly evaporate with the warmth of a rising sun. No, it is not Singer's story alone. It is also last night's dream, the private movie that somehow untangled the knots in my subconscious while I slept so I could rise this morning with new strength and courage in spite of yesterday's encroaching fear. It is also that documentary Liza and I just saw about a Japanese family rising above wartime racism to find unimagined success in America. Who can watch such a program and not be inspired, not shed tears? The strength of our fellow human beings is contagious. We must get close to certain people and do our best to get smitten by what they already have.

As for the age-old argument about evil and injustice in the world, I'm not smart enough to give an answer. I don't know why bad things happen to good people. Maybe no one does. Maybe there are certain things that are simply beyond human understanding. But when I come across an intricately designed house, I know this is the handiwork of an architect. There is not the slightest doubt. How much more convincing, then, when I behold the infinitely greater intricacy of the earth, of the universe? Our thoughts are our lives and so we had better get them in order. This is not cause for alarm; rather, it is an invitation to greater joy. The more we get our thinking in line with the positive forces around us, the more we will be able to tap into their energies and ride their waves. Negative forces, I know, are also surging nearby. It is therefore imperative that we be mindful, moment by moment, of the choices passing before us … and choose wisely. Even bad choices can teach us. I remember a *New York Times* article about Muggsy Bogues, the 5' 3" NBA star whose father was a role model for him even though the father ended up in prison; the player said he learned a lot from his father about how *not* to be. Perhaps even the negative forces are part of the Divine Plan; if we could see further into the future, we'd understand.

For hundreds of years, science has been telling us many things that seem to contradict the teachings of religion, that seem to leave no room for a spiritual dimension of life. But, lately, more and more scientists are pointing to some kind of unifying center to everything, some heretofore unknown energy that may just be the linchpin upon which everything else depends. The great spiritual masters of the world have always taught that matter is not really separate from spirit, but is simply a manifestation of it, something the physical parts of us can recognize and work with. Body and spirit are not mutually exclusive and recent discoveries support this perspective. It is no longer considered superstition to believe that all matter contains spirit, and that all spirit reveals itself, expresses itself, through the medium of matter. Judaism has always taught that we must utilize the material parts of our existence to elevate the spiritual. The most ordinary activities become sublime when we practice them with love and balance, whether it be the eating of an orange or the stacking of firewood. It is not so much the particular circumstances that determine the state of one's life as the *consciousness* with which one *lives* those circumstances. Spirit is everywhere around us if we are quiet enough to hear it, if we are humble enough to tone down our egos and simply be its channel. The line between what is spirit and what is material disappears in direct proportion to our own awakening.

Now I sit quietly in front of a computer screen, my salad eaten, a few minutes still left before the next class. I contemplate these miracles: how is it that I can recall that moment in second grade when our ball went over the fence of the school's rooftop playground and I scrambled down and out onto Kings Highway to retrieve it? How is it that my eyeball sees? How is it that I did not plan the two *balls* in those last two sentences, but they popped out of me and worked well anyway? You do not believe me? You think this is all contrived? OK, then what about that time when Jacob was a boy and he fell backwards off the boardwalk in Long Beach onto the pavement, twelve feet below, and didn't even get a scratch, let alone a broken bone? Luck, you say? Coincidence? I don't think so. I think there's something else at work in the world, every single second, that even our most advanced equipment cannot measure or substantiate. Just because you can't see something doesn't mean it isn't there.

In sixty-three years, I've learned that there are many kinds of evidence that are beyond quantification, that cannot be jotted down on some chart or punched into some calculator, and every day brings me more. Walt Whitman, that great literary mystic, once wrote: "The smallest hinge in my hand puts to scorn all machinery." Somehow, for me, this, too, is a kind of evidence. Walt's two-hundredth birthday is coming up at the end of the month and so it's fitting that his life and his writing now become part of this story, part of this *Proof*: in the final analysis, he reminds us, the smallest sprout shows there is really no death, only new growth, new life. And the force behind all this growth, all this life – this beautiful, miraculous dance between body and spirit we're forever engaged in – is God.

Peeled Garlic and Bananas

Live each hour in such a way that your memory of it will forever be a blessing lifting you up rather than a curse weighing you down.

This is primarily about memory, I think, so let me rewind the clock a bit and see if I can explain. I've been watching the Ken Burns documentary on the Roosevelts the last few days and was particularly struck, just a few minutes ago, by that famous line from FDR's first inaugural address, "The only thing we have to fear is … fear itself." I put those three dots – the marks of ellipsis I believe they're called – because Roosevelt deliberately paused there for dramatic effect. The nation was in the midst of the Great Depression at that time in the early 30's, and was desperate for leadership, for someone in government to take some kind of decisive action. Eleven years earlier, Roosevelt had suddenly been crippled by polio and most people thought his political life was over. But he found the courage to persevere, to get back into the arena, and he went on to become, some would say, the greatest US president of the twentieth century.

Few people remember, however, the rest of that famous sentence. Here it is in its entirety: *So, first of all, let me assert my firm belief that the only thing we have to fear is fear itself—nameless, unreasoning, unjustified terror which paralyzes needed efforts to convert retreat into advance.* I think it's no accident that he used the word "paralyzes" in that line. His body had been immobilized, struck down, but not his mind, not his spirit. He had personally experienced devastating fear when his legs suddenly stopped working, but he had somehow managed to climb up out of the black hole of that fear. Now he was encouraging the entire nation to do the same.

Even though all this happened before I was born, I still have memories of that critical moment in American history. There were newsreels in school, adults talking around dinner tables, remembering. The old tapes keep getting played and new ones are made every day. I guess we tune into what we're able to tune into at any given moment in our lives. The rest becomes just so much static.

If I go back in time a bit further, I see my two sons at the top of Peekamoose Mountain in the Catskills. There's a picture to preserve the memory. It wasn't an easy climb and I was especially impressed that my younger son, Adam, had made it. My older boy, Jacob, had had a friend along that particular trip, but Adam had matched them step for step. We were hours going up and hours coming down, and the icy water of the Blue Hole was like medicine for us that day.

And now, winding back still further, I'm miraculously transported to 1969, summer. I'll never forget. We had all crammed into Gloria Chiarello's bungalow to watch the moon landing. I was only thirteen and could only partially comprehend the magnitude of what I was witnessing. But I keep returning to it over the years, the memory always there for me – shifting around a bit, sure – but always there for me, finding its place among the thousands of others, all of them forever moving, coalescing, rearranging themselves – even riffing off each other – to give my life its present shape, its meaning. Who would we be without our memories?

If I reach back even further, I remember the punchball games on the roof of my second-grade yeshiva in Brooklyn, the time the ball went over the fence and down the five stories to the street below. Can I really be that same kid who ran down the stairwell that day, and out onto Kings Highway, to retrieve it? If it is true that our cells completely regenerate themselves every seven years, then which part of me is still that little kid? What is this miracle we call memory, this kaleidoscopic film of one's life that is forever being reshaped, forever edited and spliced and engineered by the deepest recesses of our subjectivity, of our souls? Certainly, it is my memory, more than anything else, that makes me feel *this* particular way, today, about myself and my world, rather than some *other* way. I'm almost afraid to think too much about it, lest its magic depart. I remember an old college professor of mine once writing, "I like to keep my past smoky, as a Yaqui wise man says we should." The same for my memory.

And now, as I peer back, again, into my own smoky depths, I see my father sprinting in from the left field of Schneider's Bungalow Colony to make another shoestring catch. A shout goes up from the crowd. Everyone I know is there, all my friends and all their parents. A beautiful little bubble of pride wells up within me (is still within me). After the game, there are cold-cut sandwiches and sodas for everyone. The lucky ones among us sit on the great boulder in the shade between the backstop and the Big Casino. Am I making this all up or do I really remember it? I'm sure about every detail except for the boulder. That one may have snuck in from some other time and place, from some other memory in my long life. But in my big picture, even the misremembered parts are true. My subconscious is the bookkeeper of my soul and is incapable of deceiving me. My own truth will out to me, no matter how much I may occasionally butcher a detail.

Perhaps this is too mystical for you. I, too, value precision, so let's talk science for a moment, shall we? A node, you may already know, is a point at which lines or pathways intersect or branch; a central or connecting point. I mention this here so that you will be somewhat ready for the following information, cut and pasted from a quick Google search: *Neurons communicate with each other at nodes called synapses. The ability of synapses to change, or remodel, themselves is called synaptic plasticity. Encoding a new long-term memory involves persistent changes in the number and shape of synapses, as well as the number of chemical messages sent and molecular docking stations, or receptors, available to receive the messages.*

Now that's all well and good, but it clarifies the miracle of memory for me about as much as a description of the eyeball clarifies the miracle of human sight. There are no words, no matter how technical or sophisticated, that are large enough, all-encompassing enough, to fully describe these miracles. To fully comprehend them, they must be lived.

And so, if we're paying attention, our minutes and days and years keep giving us everything we need to just sit back, from time to time, and watch the film of our lives, review it and think about what it is we're really doing here, take some kind of inner accounting and make sure we're on the right track. Memory is a great gift, but only if we use it to raise ourselves, to attempt tomorrow what we thought impossible today. It is never simply an accumulation of thoughts; it is always much more than that. It is a great mirror, forever reminding us of who we are, an ongoing reflection that can motivate us to change anytime we don't like what we see.

There are big memories and little memories, but somehow they all weave themselves together into the epic moving picture that is our lives, each one a sound in our song, a word in our ongoing story. Even a little thing like yesterday, when, as I was heading out the door, and I had asked my wife if she needed anything in town – even that tiny, seemingly insignificant moment has taken its unique place in my Great Tapestry. But how can I possibly convey the subtlety of this to you? How can I expect you, who have your own song, your own story, to understand? Let me try:

It was late afternoon. I was giving Adam, now eighteen, a ride to his friend's house, down east, on Monroe Boulevard. Usually, I check with Liza when I'm going somewhere with the car, see if she needs anything in town. This time, I was struck by the incongruity of her response: "Peeled garlic and bananas." I think I even told her that would be a good title for a story. But it has become far more than just that by now. That banal exchange with my wife, that simple moment in time, has found its small but indelible place in my memory, in the holiday dinner we had, just a few nights later, to usher in the New Year, that one moment now joined to all the other moments, the effect of their joining intricate and beautiful, like the beads of a cherished necklace hanging over your heart.

We had gathered in the living room for a while, family and friends, remembering past times, past celebrations, all that *life* we had shared together over the decades. Soon, the smells drew us to table. We spoke some words of prayer, then headed into the kitchen for the beautiful buffet. I can still see it now: giant platters of food all artfully laid out – a visual feast before you even took a bite! Everything looked so tempting, my plate was almost full by the time I got to the last dish, the one all the way on the right of the counter. The aroma of that mashed cauliflower, primarily the garlic in it, wafted into my nose and was soon on my tongue. The sounds of the words, the taste of the food, the power of the prayer, the love of the people that holiday night are now forever within me, shaping me, shifting and stirring and marinating in my Great Bowl, the ever-revolving, ever-expanding container of memory.

The Better Angel of my Nature

Way back when I was a kid, a typical Baby Boomer suburban kid who probably saw every *Loony Tunes* cartoon ever created, I remember seeing those two balloons pop up on either side of Bugs Bunny's head every time he was faced with a tough decision between doing the right thing and doing the selfish thing. The balloon on the left, you may recall, contained a devilish-looking character who tried to convince Bugs to forget every consideration except his own selfish desire. The balloon on the right contained an angelic-looking character who did precisely the opposite, imploring Bugs to think of the deeper consequences of the choice he was about to make, to get outside himself a bit and see the bigger, higher picture within which he was, at that precise moment, living. Cartoons were a primary source of information for me back then, young sponge that I was. Years later, some guy would write a book entitled, *All I Really Need to Know I Learned in Kindergarten*; he sure got that right.

But even if we *did* learn everything we really need to know in kindergarten, those early lessons would eventually need deepening, a more nuanced teaching one could apply to unimagined, sometimes baffling situations. So I kept listening to the cues my culture was giving me. In one episode of *The Honeymooners*, an old couple unexpectedly shows up at Ralph and Alice's door, explaining that they had lived in that apartment decades before, when they were first starting out, wondering if they could come in and see it again. When Ralph learns that the husband is the owner of a famous, successful business, he asks him if there is some secret to his success. The old man replies that one day, in that very room, he had made a list of all his good characteristics and all his bad characteristics and resolved that he would work diligently at building up the good ones and eliminating the bad ones. He followed through with this plan and became a huge success. Of course, as soon as the couple leaves, Ralph decides he will draw up these lists as well. He immediately throws himself into a no-holds-barred program of self-reformation, driving Alice absolutely crazy in the process, but, as usual, ends up failing miserably.

Judaism famously requires each of its adherents to practice some deep self-analysis during the "Ten Days of Repentance," the special interval of time between the holy days of Rosh Hashanah and Yom Kippur. Less well known is the fact that such an accounting is expected of Jews every single day, preferably before bedtime. The idea is that by honestly reviewing how we have comported ourselves in the immediate past, we will be better equipped to make changes, to improve ourselves as we move into the future. Although we are all born with that non-material, essential part of us called the soul, it's up to each one us what we do with it. We can build it up through good deeds so that it shines brighter and eases our way forward, or we can darken its light with the shame and regret accrued through poor choices. Each day presents new opportunities.

Our films and books and plays are filled with the idea of personal growth, of self-improvement, of an individual's choice between the two roads that almost perpetually lie ahead of him. Sometimes the choice is as simple as whether he should have that second cookie he's had his eye on, but sometimes it's a bit murkier.

The other day, at work in my present capacity as a substitute teacher, I happened to be paired with a science teacher who was nothing less than toxic to his students. He was bullying them and frightening them, not teaching them. I had never witnessed anything like this in my thirty-two years in the classroom and decided I must go see the principal about it. I felt a professional and moral obligation to blow the whistle on this guy. I could not in good conscience do nothing. But I knew that going to the principal could entail some serious consequences – not only for the teacher, but also for me – and so I decided to wait and think the situation through before doing anything.

A little later that day, I was handing out some work booklets, following very specific instructions from the absent teacher. All of a sudden, this frenetic woman bursts into the room and starts grabbing the booklets back from the students, telling me I shouldn't have handed them out. I try to explain that I was following explicit instructions that had been left for me, but she would have none of it (I think she was the Teacher's Assistant for that classroom). When the bell rang, she told me that the booklet was the "fun" part of the lesson and students were supposed to complete their other work first. The regular teacher had not stipulated that in her instructions and so I had no way of knowing. Despite my explanation, she probably just thought I was a fool.

An hour or so later, I happened to see her in the hall, talking to two other adults I assume were teachers. Before she saw me, I overheard her say something about this "substitute handing out the fun booklets before the work" and realized I was the subject of her gossip. I immediately remembered my intention to go report the teacher who had bullied the students and felt as though the hand of God were tapping me on the shoulder, giving me pause: just as this woman was presenting her colleagues with a completely distorted picture of who I truly was, how did I know I was not about to do the very same thing with the science teacher? It's been a couple weeks now and I haven't said anything yet. Maybe I'll speak with the teacher directly instead of reporting him; I'm not sure yet what I'll do. But at least I've taken a step back and am more thoughtful about the whole thing now than I might have been had this little hallway encounter not occurred. I still have this choice life has placed before me. I could choose to think primarily about protecting myself; I could do nothing. But there are sins of omission as well commission and so I'm still considering taking some kind of action on behalf of those innocent kids. On the other hand, maybe there's more to this picture than met my eye. So I'm going to take my time with this; I'm going to take a deep breath.

Around twenty-five years ago, I did a "Vision Quest" with a bunch of guys up in the Adirondacks, not far from Lake Placid. It was a wonderful ten-day camping trip during which we practiced various North American Indian rituals designed to push the participant out of his comfort zone, to break through old, self-imposed limits and maybe emerge into some newer, better self. I remember this one guy named Hubbs whose wonderfully savage scream would break the stillness of the woods just before his body broke the stillness of the ice-cold river he dove into each morning. He once told me to "live each day as though it were your last." We discussed how this attitude would make every moment more precious, the taste of food more rich, the touch of a friend more miraculous.

Lately, I've been thinking about those words Hubbs spoke to me. I guess we get a little smarter over the years and we begin to realize that admonitions such as this one need not make us anxious. We don't need to tighten up at the thought that every moment counts. On the contrary, we can loosen up, relax, knowing that, because every moment is crucial, every single one of them is needed, even the ones we *think* we wasted. They weren't *really* wasted; every one of them was needed to get us where we are. If we hold our head right, even our bad choices can help us progress. One time, I found a brand-new football in a park just as the sun was setting. I looked around for the owner, but everyone was gone; it was just me, my wife and my two young boys. I figured, "finders keepers, losers weepers," but Liza had another think coming for me. She said I should leave it right where I found it, that the person who left it might be returning. I still aspire to her level of honesty.

Our choices will keep materializing before us, the bubbles of angel and devil hovering over our heads. There are people, I guess, who go through a lifetime without much struggle; they don't hesitate at all. Self-reflection is an alien concept to them and they'd probably scoff at the notion of someone taking a daily accounting of his soul. I'm not sure if they're truly blessed or truly cursed. In any case, I'm glad I have Liza at my side, and Hubbs, and every friend or relative or stranger who ever woke me from my dozing with their screams or with their whispers, helped nudge me forward along my path.

Maybe I'll never be able to go on autopilot, but maybe I'm not really supposed to; I'm supposed to remain alert for what comes next. There *is* a way to toe that magical line between high alert and deep calm, a way to drink life's cup to the dregs without tasting any of the stress. It ain't easy, but it's doable. It's probably something akin to what the old coach said to his beloved players in the final seconds of their crucial game: "Be quick, but don't hurry." Over time, little by little, I'm getting better at figuring out precisely what that means. I've even begun to use the little bit I already understand to inform the precious seconds of *my* game. Lately, when I take an accounting of my soul at the end of the day, the better angel of my nature, forever hovering there above me, is smiling, knowing that not one drop of his prodding has been in vain.

Living in The Buffer Zone

When my father started teaching me how to drive, I distinctly remember him telling me, repeatedly, "You have to keep a buffer zone all around you." What he meant was, that when you're operating a motor vehicle, it's important to keep a safe distance not only between you and whatever's in *front* of you, but also between you and whatever's on the other three sides. One might argue that advice to stay away from the guy in front of you is reasonable because you can control that particular distance simply by slowing down, but suggesting that you have any control over the guy behind you or the drivers on either side is ridiculous; what control do you have there? However, a little more consideration of the matter will yield a different conclusion: by continuously scanning all three of your mirrors and making subtle adjustments with the controls that *are* at your disposal, you can avoid getting too close to drivers on *any* side, regardless of what surprise moves they may make.

Lately, I'm beginning to apply this advice to life *off* the road as well. Although we're often presented with baffling choices, there's a balance to be found in just about everything, a buffer zone within which we can operate, a forever shifting space – relatively small, yes – but still big enough to allow for some wiggle room. There is an art to moving safely and gracefully within this space, and it takes a lifetime to learn it … maybe *more* than one. I know a lot more today than I did yesterday, but I'm still learning how to negotiate the tricky curves of this life, still accruing lessons on how to maneuver safely and happily within the spaces presented to me.

This buffer zone idea could be compared to a kind of scale upon which we place all the challenges that confront us in an ongoing attempt to arrive at some sort of equilibrium. We weigh everything on this scale – from how much food to heap onto our plates at an all-you-can-eat buffet to how much humility we should practice before people misconstrue our intentions and treat us like doormats. It's amazing how one concept can be so universally applicable.

Take time, for instance. I read somewhere, "Time can be your enemy or your friend." I have always been very punctual, something I also learned from my father. But, lately, I'm realizing that, by increasing the size of my time buffer zone just a bit more, I can increase the quality of my life. Things often manage to get in the way of any plan, no matter how simple and well designed. By leaving myself a little extra time for unforeseen circumstances, not only am I more relaxed on my way to whatever it is I'm about to do, but I'm also more able to fully enjoy it once I get there. If this precaution ends up having been unnecessary, I simply kick back and read the book I've intentionally brought along – something I enjoy anyway. Being too early is never a problem if you're ready for it; being late takes away all your options.

Money is another one of those major thoroughfares in life that can work for you or against you, depending on how well you've developed a buffer zone for it. Mine is still evolving … has been since eighth grade, when I delivered *Newsday* after school and earned my first paychecks. I remember my contact man giving me a little green booklet to keep track of my accounts. Eventually, jobs at a book store, a supermarket, a hotel, and a camp allowed me to squirrel away enough money to pay for three of my first four years of college; after dad paid for freshman year, I realized he had enough on his plate with three other kids and a mortgage, so I told myself it was time to start chipping in. He appreciated my thinking this way and, one day, after I paid back an unrelated debt I owed him, on time, he left me a note on the kitchen counter saying, "Your credit with me is good up to $100,000." All my experiences with money over the years have taught me a very simple lesson: don't spend beyond what you already have in your pocket. I'm reminded of that line in *Walden* by Thoreau: "The fruits eaten temperately need not make us ashamed of our appetites. But put an extra condiment into your dish, and it will poison you." When I was in my thirties, these lines spoke to me especially forcefully because I had an eating disorder. Today, that particular compulsion fully healed, I'm able to think about the words "temperately" and "extra" as they can be applied to activities *other* than eating. Moderation in all things is certainly good advice. And "extra," I now see, means "too much," no matter how negligible I rationalize some new and present "extra" to be.

You get to a certain point in your life when things start converging. Old experiences that didn't seem to fit into any recognizable category begin to take their proper place in the bigger picture; meaning evolves. I'm seeing the advantage of keeping a buffer zone now in just about everything I do – and it's not at all about being pessimistic or paranoid; it's about optimizing my short time here on this blessed earth, making the most of my days, minute by minute, to the very best of my ability. Never *mind* that the other guy stops short or drifts out of his lane for no reason! The question isn't, "Why did he do that?" It's, "How *ready* was I for what he did?" or, "What adjustment do *I* need to make so I'll be ready the next time?"

These days, I take the dog to the beach every morning and throw a ball for him to do his sprints and his digging, but I try to be cognizant of our relative distance to the water; otherwise, the ocean will swallow it as though it were a fat latke. Before we leave the house, I do a few stretches, keeping in mind the mantras of old high school coaches. One always said, "No pain, no gain." The other, "Use pain as an *indicator*" (for knowing when to *stop*). Somewhere between these two competing guidelines, I find my deepest stretch – a position that's difficult for me to reach, but not quite so extreme that I end up hurting myself.

Back in the 80's, Mayor Giuliani instituted a new policing program called "Broken Windows." Now, I'm a pretty liberal guy, but if something makes sense and it's fair, I'm all for it. The rationale was that by cracking down on the smallest of crimes, people would get the message that there was a new sheriff in town and they'd better beware. The policy was a huge success; crime rates throughout the city dropped dramatically. I'd been doing a version of this policy with my students for years; if you give people too much license, some of them will take advantage, and we all end up paying the cost. I guess, sometimes, a *smaller* buffer zone is just what the doctor ordered.

I have lots of other memories I can share with you to exemplify this idea that, even though we can't control what happens around us, we *can* control the depth of our own preparation and the efficacy of our own response. For now, let me leave you with this one: when I was a kid in yeshiva, the rabbis would often exhort us to "build a fence around the Torah." We knew that building a fence meant doing even more than was required in the performance of a *mitzvah,* a good deed, in order to ensure its proper execution, regardless of any obstacles we might encounter. If doing a *mitzvah* could elevate one, as we'd been taught, then going the extra mile in performance of that *mitzvah,* making the *mitzvah* buffer zone wider to safeguard its optimal completion, could raise one even higher.

It's a comforting feeling to know that I can shift my scales, that I can increase or decrease the buffer zone between the world and me any time I choose. It's not a *lot* of control, I agree, but it's all I have, and I want to embrace it, utilize it, as much as is humanly possible. Things still happen that displease me, of course, but my displeasure is minimized, knowing that I've done everything in my power to be part of my own solution rather than part of my own problem. I think I'm getting better at this art of keeping a buffer zone. People tell me I'm smiling much more now than I used to and, lately, it feels like I have much more time to stop along the road and just enjoy the scenery. It's a very long journey I'm traveling and it's *so* beautiful; I don't want to focus *too* much on my destination … just enough.

Just Before Sunrise

Snickers is our almost-seven-year-old Rhodesian Ridgeback/Black Mouth Cur mix. The cops in Long Beach are super-strict about dogs on the beach; they'll write a ticket quick as look at you. So, for years, first thing in the morning, I would drive all the way down to the local dog run – almost a fifteen-minute ride – let him do his business, clean it up, then wing his favorite ball five or six times in the adjacent soccer field. About a year ago, some guy told me the cops don't start their dog patrol until seven in the morning; we immediately switched our routine to the beach and have been enjoying it ever since.

I say, "enjoying," but I should probably qualify that. In the novel, *The Yearling*, one of my favorite lines is spoken by the father, Penny, to his young son, Jody, who has just returned home after mistakenly thinking his parents had betrayed him. The boy had gone three days and nights without any food and Penny knew he needed comfort, but he needed honesty too. So the father said to his son: "Life is fine – *powerful* fine – but it ain't easy."

He sure got that right. My morning trip to the beach with Snickers is the toughest thing I do, physically, every day. It's way tougher than my regular workouts at the local recreation center where I do some rigorous stretches in the steam room, push myself fairly hard in the pool, and finish with twenty-five crunches and leg raises on the deck. Now that I think about it, it's tough mentally, too. I mean, there's a lot involved.

You might ask, "What's the big deal about going to the beach with your dog? How much can that possibly *involve*?" But there's actually quite a bit involved, a lot of *life* packed into *everything* we do, even a seemingly insignificant thing like a walk on a beach. I want to see the importance of every moment in my life, suck out every drop of its juice. I want to give my dog, and myself, the best possible start to the day. And, anyway, who's to say, with any certainty, which of our moments is more significant than any other? If we look carefully, the ordinary moments don't seem so ordinary after a while. Let me tell you about my morning jaunts with Snickers.

I get up and out from under two warm blankets at around 5:30 or so, fill his two indoor bowls with food and water, the outdoor one with just water, then gather all the little items experience has taught me to bring along: a thin pair of gloves, half of a treat, and a couple poop bags. Next, I do a few yoga positions, release some of the tightness accrued in sleep; Snickers likes to move way faster than I do at that hour, and I've learned to be ready for him. Of course, I could just ignore his pulling and force him to go at my pace. But I know he can't wait to get to the beach, and so I try to accommodate him as much as I can. After all, the faster pace is good for me too … provided I've limbered up enough to avoid a muscle pull; I've recently discovered I'm not eighteen anymore. But whether I'm eighteen or sixty-four, the advice of my old high school coach still applies: "Be quick, but don't hurry."

In addition to old muscles that don't particularly feel like sprinting first thing in the morning, there's also the temperature: the other day was 17 degrees, if you include the infamous wind-chill factor (as I understand it, when you're outside, and it's windy, you have no choice but to include it). Although I'm able to slow down once we get to the beach and I take off his leash, I still need to jog around quite a bit to make sure the distance between us remains manageable; occasionally, another early-bird human will be out at that special hour, just before sunrise, and, although Snickers loves people, a strange, eighty-pound, wild-looking animal loping toward you in the pre-dawn light could give you a heart attack before you've had a chance to learn all he'd wanted to do was show you his precious ball.

But, most of the time, it's just the two of us. After he relieves himself and I bag it, I make sure to give him at least five throws before we head back home. I have one of those special sticks that enable you to wing a ball much farther than you ever could unassisted; my best throws probably go sixty or seventy yards. Oh, yeah, something else I forgot to tell you makes it a bit challenging first in the morning: we're out there so early, there's barely enough *light* to keep track of the ball once it leaves the cradle at the end of the stick. Luckily, the ball is designed with little holes in it, and the whistling it makes in flight helps Snickers stay on its track. But not always.

Sometimes the wind drowns out the whistle and I have to run up there with him and make sure he gets it before some seagull or aberrant wave distracts him and he decides to run off and play without me. Usually, though, he stays right on its course, watching its flight as he sprints, then dives the last few yards, front paws outstretched, the sand exploding in every direction as he pounces on it. He then runs back toward me, and I encourage him by yelling, "Good boy!" and, once he's close enough, in a much softer voice, "Stay here," pointing with the end of the stick to the hole he had started after the first throw; I usually do two throws before allowing him the relative respite of digging.

When he gets the gentle command, he'll drop the ball and dig a little hole right next to it; gravity pulls it in. Then, he'll keep digging, the ball sinking deeper and deeper. Sometimes, his paw will accidentally enclose the ball and it'll fly up and out, rolling several feet away. He'll immediately pounce on it, retrieve it, and drop it back into the hole. I'll let him enjoy this game for a while, the hole evolving into a crater, until he's caught his breath; then I'll wing it again and our dance continues.

After he's chased five or six throws, I'll get the ball away from him, replace my heavy mittens with the thin gloves, and clean as much of the sand as I can out of his mouth. I then pick up the poop bag I left over by the dune while we played and head for home. Back on our porch, I'll break up the half-a treat into four pieces and drop them, one at a time, into the water bowl I'd filled earlier. I'll watch as he dunks his entire muzzle each time. This gets rid of most of whatever sand remains in or around his mouth; before I learned this little trick, he would sometimes puke from having swallowed too much beach.

As I said at the outset, this is the toughest part of my day, but it's totally worth it. For one thing, there's a great sense of relief knowing that, whatever I encounter in the rest of my day, it'll be nothing compared to this; the trail feels all downhill from here. For another, Snickers is like a great athlete whose body needs to *move*. If I were a great athlete cooped up in a house all day, I would certainly appreciate someone letting me out to run on a beach. In fact, the Torah *requires* us to feed our animals before we feed ourselves. Although one could argue that this is simply because, thousands of years ago, we relied on animals to help us farm and get our food, I think there's much more to it than that. I think the main intention of this law is to inculcate the unnatural habit of putting others, even animals, before ourselves. Somehow, though it's counter intuitive, this level of generosity also ends up being an especially effective recipe for *self*-care.

Jody's father had told him, "Life is fine - *powerful* fine - but it ain't easy." I like that he put the *fine* part before the *ain't easy* part. I don't think that was an accident. We learn, as we walk the road of this long and long life, that there are no short cuts, that what we get out of each day is equal to what we put into it, each day contributing to the overall Sculpture, each moment leaving our fingerprints on the Clay.

My mornings with Snickers are anything but easy, but I will continue with every bit of the work and every bit of the fun. I often tell my students that the lessons we encounter in literature are not lessons you can just learn once and fully get. They're lessons that need to be learned over and over again, lessons I'm *still* learning, together with them, even though I may have taught the same book twenty times. Maybe living life is like making art, like music: it takes lots of practice to play well.

Last Saturday, I had an old Wurlitzer piano delivered to my son Jacob's room. The former owners had been a little bit at odds over what to do with it: the husband wanted more room in their house, but the wife was still way too attached to it to give it up; eventually, she agreed to let it go and I was able to call the movers and give them the green light.

For weeks, I had given this little project of mine to find my son a piano the same attention to detail I give to my morning jaunts with Snickers. I think back now to a long-ago trip to Japan, the tea ceremony I witnessed there one day in which every movement was slowed down enough, intentional enough, to approach something like meditation, something one might even call sacred. I'm trying to move through my life in this way, trying to do the work given to me as mindfully as I possibly can.

Dave, the piano tuner, seems like the kind of guy who embraces his work, too; he was in there with his tools for at least two hours, said it was in great shape for an old spinet, but that it probably hadn't been tuned in over fifty years. It sure sounds amazing now, though. Jacob will be thrilled when he gets home from school; I never let on that all this was happening: he knew about my *general* plan, but had no idea it was nearing fruition. I can't wait to see the expression on his face when he walks into his bedroom and sees that long line of black and white keys where his desk used to be.

I guess maybe each of us, as we get older, is a little like that old piano: there's still plenty of fine music waiting to come out of us, but we need to constantly tune ourselves, constantly adjust the internal hammers and strings of our minds and our bodies for optimal balance, optimal performance. There's no end to the lessons or the tunings, no easy switch we can simply flip and be done with it, no way we can just sit back and rest on our laurels. It's a lot of work and, sometimes, it's really hard, but it's all worth it in the end, isn't it? I mean, I *could* just walk Snickers around the block every morning, but then my life, which is inextricably linked with the lives of so many others, wouldn't quite be what I want it to be. So, instead, I'll keep paying the price, keep doing the work I've been blessed with, and keep repeating that mantra, over and over again, give myself some strength, some encouragement: "Life is fine - *powerful* fine – but it ain't easy."

Ambition

In the great 1954 classic, *On the Waterfront,* there's that memorable scene when the two brothers, Johnny and Terry, are in the back seat of a car, talking to each other. The older brother, Johnny, has just been instructed by the mob boss to make sure Terry isn't thinking about testifying against them. He tries to convince his younger brother that he's hanging out too much on his own, that he needs to get back in the loop, stay more connected with the mob, think about his future: "It's time to think about getting some ambition," he says. "I always figured I'd live a little bit longer without it," Terry replies.

That response has always resonated with me. Terry was probably thinking not only about the *length* of his life but also about the *quality* of his life. Reminds me of that Emerson quote ... something along the lines of: "It is infinitely preferable that my life be of *substance* than that it glitter." Thoreau put it this way: "How many a poor immortal soul have I met well-nigh crushed and smothered under its load, creeping down the road of life, pushing before it a barn seventy-five feet by forty, its Augean stables never cleansed, and one hundred acres of land, tillage, mowing, pasture, and wood-lot. The portionless, who struggle with no such unnecessary inherited encumbrances, find it labor enough to subdue and cultivate a few cubic feet of flesh."

Although certainly not identical, these two statements are saying basically the same thing: ambition can be dangerous if you're not careful with your aim. If we're always chasing money or looking to grow our material possessions in order to feel good about ourselves, we're fighting a losing battle. I often hear myself telling students that we are mind, body and spirit and that these parts of us need exercising every single day. Of course, money and material things are a necessary part of life, but so many people lose their way by making them more important than they actually are. If you're concerned about keeping up with the Joneses more than you're concerned with ... keeping your body fit, for example, then you've got your priorities mixed up. Finding a balance between competing forces isn't always easy, especially when each one is so attractive.

Self-care vs. caring for others, for example; it's hard to know where to draw the line. A long time ago, way back in my freshman year at SUNY Fredonia, I enrolled in a water safety/lifeguarding class to learn how to swim properly. I was surprised that the very first thing they taught us was how to get *away* from a drowning victim. The idea is that, if a victim panics and grabs you around the neck, you need to know how to escape quickly; otherwise, two people can end up drowning instead of one. Hopefully, by getting away and regrouping, you can then swim back for another try, warn the victim not to grab you, that you're there to help. There's nothing wrong with taking good care of yourself when your ultimate goal is helping others; sometimes, it's even necessary to put yourself first in order to be in a position where you can make a greater contribution. But if your ego is what's driving you, if you're looking to glitter and shine just so others will notice how big your barn has become, you're misplacing your energy.

The divine law of compensation is not a personal savings account; it is a *global* account in which everyone has a stake. The Torah teaches us that we must practice *tikun olam,* "repairing the world," but, to do this, our ambition must be pointed in the right direction. Concentrating on our own few feet of cubic flesh is a good beginning; we *should* keep ourselves healthy by carving out some quality time for ourselves; we should *enjoy* our possessions and make sure they are always simple enough to remain a joy rather than a burden. But if we intend to participate in the greater cause of *tikun olam,* we must do far more than that. We must cultivate the kind of ambition that encourages us to shine more *within* than without, the kind informed by the perspective that putting ourselves first is a certainly a good strategy … but only insofar as it gives us what we need to better serve the others living with us in our small sphere of the wider world.

Luck

Sometime around the end of 1985 or the beginning of 1986, I can't remember exactly, I was sitting in my apartment on 121st Street and Broadway in Manhattan, flipping through a newspaper; it was either *The New York Post* or *The Daily News*. The words "300 Teachers Needed" in large bold type caught my eye and I started reading the fine print. Apparently, New York City was experiencing a shortage of licensed educators and the Board of Ed. had put together a special hiring hall downtown where anyone interested in a city job was invited to apply the following Monday. Years later, my wife would often remark that I'm a very lucky person. I agree with her. But I also think luck is not the whole story. It's just like that old joke about two guys debating whether it's destiny or free will that controls our lives: they're so engrossed in what they're saying, they don't even notice that the light has changed and that they're in the middle of a busy intersection. They look up just in time to see a huge bus bearing down on them; they both run for the sidewalk. How is this like luck not being the whole story? We'll see.

I had been attending a college called The Jewish Theological Seminary of America for the previous year-and-a-half or so with the idea of getting a second Masters and maybe teaching Jewish Studies one day. But at the moment I saw that advertisement in the paper, I was forcefully struck with the realization that, at twenty-nine years of age, I was still sharing a bathroom with three other guys, I was always broke, and I had never really had a place I could call my own; I decided to head downtown Monday and show up at that hiring hall.

Even though I made sure to arrive early, the place was packed; it was like a zoo: lines and lines of people waiting to fill out endless forms. There must have been at least fifteen hundred people vying for those three hundred jobs. On the last of the many lines, we were told to return Wednesday to complete the process. As I handed in my paperwork to an older woman sitting behind the table, something made me lean over and ask if there was any way I could avoid the lines on Wednesday. She whispered something and I had to ask her to repeat herself. She again whispered, "Come back tomorrow."

I walked into an empty hall the next day. The same lady took my papers, stamped them, and told me to see a Mr. Rufus Thomas in Room 418. Mr. Thomas instructed me to take the subway to Wingate High School in Brooklyn for an interview and that I would most likely be hired on the spot. I met with Dennis Branscum in a little closet-like office that also served as a book room. After telling me I had the job, he asked how Nat was doing. I asked him who Nat was and he replied, "Your Uncle!" During the eleven and-a-half years I worked in Wingate's English department, I don't think anybody there ever believed that, until the day of that interview, I had had no idea my Uncle Natie was the English Chairperson at Wingate until he retired and Dennis took the job. To this day, they probably think Natie pulled some strings for me. He did not; until Dennis told me about this secular part of my Uncle's life, Natie had always been someone I knew only as a Rabbi, and as one of my father's four older brothers.

Seven years later, in September of 1993, a few of the other veteran teachers and I were showing the new hires around the neighborhood. We brought them over to Master Lou's bakery and a few of the other local eateries Wingate teachers frequented for a quick bite on a free period. I immediately noticed a very pretty young lady among them, but not enough time had passed from a recent break-up for me to think of asking anyone out yet.

A couple months later, that young lady – Lisa or Liza, I couldn't quite remember her name – popped into my head on a Saturday afternoon. I made up my mind to find her and ask her out; I hadn't seen her once since that day we met and was hoping she hadn't been reassigned. When I got into the English office on Monday, I asked Gurlynne, one of the new teachers who was with us that day we walked over to Master Lou's, if Lisa/Liza was still working at Wingate. She said, yes, *Liza* was, but that she always ate lunch in one of the art rooms so she'd have time to grade her students' bulky projects and not have to carry them home on the subway; that's probably why I hadn't seen her since September.

During seventh period that day, I walked down to the art hall and found her alone at her desk in the front of the room (she later told me one student had been in the back, drawing). We had a short but sweet conversation and she agreed to see me one day "outside the building." Later that afternoon, at a faculty meeting, we passed a single sheet of paper between us, like two students passing love notes. We agreed to meet up that Thursday, right after school, and take a walk in Prospect Park.

There was a little snow on the ground that day – enough to make our walk beautiful, but not enough to make it difficult. Afterwards, we had a quiet dinner at a Chinese restaurant in Park Slope. Liza bought a Chanukah menorah at a little shop near the subway. We kissed for the first time just before she headed down the stairs for her train. This was on December 2nd.

Liza kept getting pink slips at the end of each school year because she had initially been hired to cover the classes of someone on sabbatical and he had returned; although they kept rehiring her, there was always the danger she'd be let go. Fortunately, after just a few months of searching for a more secure job, she landed a tenure-track position at Malverne Middle School; things were looking up.

Unfortunately, things at Wingate were deteriorating. One day, a bullet went through a guidance counselor's window; there was some kind of a gang war going on outside and two kids were shot. When Liza heard about it, she said I should get the hell out of there. I immediately started sending my resumé to every district on Long Island. After a few weeks of rejections, I got lucky and was hired to teach at Great Neck South High School. This was several months before the end of the school year in 1997 and I wanted to do the right thing and inform Dennis I wouldn't be coming back in September. When I told him where I was headed, he said, "You'll be back; those Great Neck parents will eat you alive." Now, Dennis Branscum was a really great boss, a super-smart guy, and a good person, but he was wrong about Great Neck. I taught there for twenty-one years and I can count on one hand how many difficult parents I encountered. Sometimes one must ignore the naysayers and hold onto one's own faith.

Liza and I were married on August 25th, 1996, a little less than three years after that first walk we took together in Prospect Park. We bought our home a little over a year later, and slept there (in sleeping bags) for the very first time on the fourth anniversary of that first date: December 2nd, 1997. Jacob was born the following September and Adam in April of 2001.

I often think back to that moment in that hiring hall, years ago, when that woman whispered, "Come back tomorrow." What if I hadn't bothered to ask her about avoiding the lines? What if she hadn't given me that wonderful tip? If I had simply returned on Wednesday instead of Tuesday, would I have still gotten the job at Wingate? Would I have ever met Liza? Would my kids have been born? I know one could ask these questions about any of the dominos in our lives; a cynic would probably just laugh at me.

But I like to think back on my days, the interesting confluence of events and people that shaped me, that brought me to my presents. As I said earlier, Liza always tells me I'm a very lucky person and I agree with her. But I also think it's important to do your best in this life, to be careful with whatever you happen to be doing at any given moment, to be as precise as possible, and not rely on luck. I guess I feel the same way Hemingway's Santiago feels, all alone in his small skiff on the wide sea, when he tells himself: "It is better to be lucky. But I would rather be exact. Then when luck comes you are ready."

This is what I was getting at before, when I said that luck not being the whole story is like that argument the two guys were having about free will vs. destiny. Maybe free will can't work without a little bit of destiny and maybe destiny can't work without a little bit of free will either. I'm not smart enough to know how this can be, but I feel it in my gut. And I'm not going to sit around waiting until I'm sure it's true. I'm going to be as careful as I can right now with my life. Sometimes, that will mean asking a secretary in a hiring hall if there's any way to avoid the lines on Wednesday; and, sometimes, it will mean running like hell for the sidewalk.

Rules Are Made To Be Broken

I don't really agree with that, although I *do* break rules sometimes. Rules are made to keep people in line, I know, but I think it's important that we're not so locked into blindly following everything we're told that we become the kind of automatons who can force people into gas chambers and later claim we were "just following orders." That's a pretty heavy start for what I hope will actually turn out to be a relatively light piece of writing. My intention is to tell you about a few memorable moments in my life when I chose to break the rules. I'm not quite ready to say I'm proud of what I did those times, but I'm certainly not ashamed.

When I was in seventh or eighth grade, I had a paper route in an apartment building one block away from my school. I was supposed to walk the one block, deliver my papers, and meet my mom in front of the building for a ride home. One day – I don't know where the idea came from – I decided to secretly cut out of school early. I snuck into the utility room bordering the beach, climbed through a window, and dropped myself down to the boardwalk below. I enjoyed complete freedom for an hour or so, then delivered the papers as usual and met my mom. Everything seemed to go flawlessly. The next day, I was called into the principal's office where my mom was waiting for me with a very stern look on her face; I was suspended for three days.

Almost immediately after my freshman year of college, my older brother, Bobby, and I spent a year working on a kibbutz in Israel. One night, very late – it must've been around twelve or one in the morning – we decided to head for the communal bakery and make ourselves some chocolate chip cookies. After an hour or so, when the cookies were out and cooling on the counter, one of us noticed the giant milk truck parked nearby; the kibbutz had cows and, although we'd never paid much attention, we knew the truck came and went frequently. We decided to give it a shot. We grabbed the cookies, still warm and smelling unreal, and climbed the silver ladder to the top of the truck. One of us, using both hands, turned the big wheel that opened the hatch. I rolled up my right sleeve to the shoulder and reached a cup down into the darkness below; unbelievably, the cup came up filled and cold as ice. The three of us sat up there in the moonlight a long time, eating and drinking and knowing we'd climbed to heaven.

A few years later, I took a trip out to California with my younger brother, Steve. We rented a car and had a fantastic time camping up in the north, but, on our way back, we were almost completely broke. When we saw the sign for San Simeon/Hearst Castle, we knew it would probably be something we couldn't afford, but we pulled in for a look anyway. Sure enough, they had a bus parked outside the property's border and it was something like twenty-two dollars to get on; that was the price of admission. I asked the worker there in the parking lot if anyone had ever gotten in for free. He said, "It's never been done." Steve and I looked at each other and silently, simultaneously, accepted the challenge. We got on the bus as though we were regular patrons, but then scooted down in the back so that when the driver came around to collect the money, he never saw us. We joined the others for the three-hour tour and were never caught. Hearst Castle is certainly worth the price of admission, even if you have to pay it.

I still don't agree that rules are made to be broken, and I do still break them occasionally. Of course, I'm a little more discriminating now than I was back in the seventh grade, and I'm never completely broke anymore, but I still manage to find situations in which I choose to rebel. Usually, these days, my rebellion *is* something I'm proud of. I guess I see it as something like being proud of walking the road less traveled; it's never an easy thing to do, but sometimes it's exactly the *right* thing to do: striking out for unmapped territory, blazing your own trail, following the dictates of your own vision, even when doing so directly contradicts the Powers That Be. I wouldn't want a youngster to read this; he might get the wrong idea. Like *Kabbalah*, certain things are dangerous unless you have enough years under your belt to handle them. I'm not arrogant enough to equate my personal philosophy with *Kabbalah*, just rebellious enough to take a shot sometimes.

Rejection

When it came time for me to start sending out applications for college, my guidance counselor told me there weren't many schools that would accept me because of my low GPA. I remember filling out one application that allowed you to list four schools. I didn't want to try for a second group of four because that would cost another twenty-five bucks. In addition, I figured if one of the first four didn't accept me, there was no reason to think anyone else would; I was already fishing at the bottom of the barrel. My high school GPA was slightly below 80.

SUNY Fredonia accepted me as a Liberal Arts major and I began to take my schoolwork seriously for the first time in my life. For years, I had seen my father working his ass off to keep us four kids clothed and fed, and I didn't want one drop of the money he was shelling out for me to be wasted; I really worked hard.

One day, I noticed a sign posted in The Union that Alan Ginsberg was going to be giving a reading and visiting some English classes. Although I was still years away from declaring myself an English major, I loved to read and I knew that Ginsberg was an important figure. I knew he had hung out with Bob Dylan and Jack Kerouac and that people considered him one of the founding members of what came to be known as "the Beat Generation." I don't think I had ever read one of his poems at that point, but he was definitely someone that a nascent hippie like me was attracted to.

When the day of his visit arrived, I hung around the English Department with a bunch of other kids and, when we spotted him leaving one of the classrooms there, walked with him as he made his way to the cafeteria. I had waited patiently to ask him something about the meditation he practiced – so many others were bombarding him with questions or sticking notebooks in his hand to autograph – and he happened to be in the middle of answering me when we got to the door of the cafeteria. Everybody else stayed outside, but his voice and his eye kind of invited me in. We ended up having lunch together and, afterwards, continued our conversation alone in the dorm room the college had provided him.

We sat on a Turkish rug he'd unrolled and he taught me a simple meditation involving the in-breath and the out-breath. He ended our session with the ringing of a Buddhist bell. I remember thinking, as we sat on that little rug and he rang that little bell, that the dorm room seemed to have been transformed into a little temple. That night, a group of us accompanied him downtown to one of the local bars. Someone lit up a joint on the way and we all passed it around. It was an incredible experience. The next day, I wrote a one-page tribute to him entitled, "Letter to a Famous Poet.

Almost twenty years later, I took my high-school class to hear him read at Brooklyn College. I brought along the tribute, thinking maybe I'd get a chance to hand it to him sometime during the day. I didn't really give it much thought, but then, during the question-and-answer session following the reading, someone got up and read what was essentially a tribute. This was my opportunity. I raised my hand, and, thinking it was more polite to preface what I was about to read in some way instead of just beginning, I said something like, "Mr. Ginsberg, I met you up at SUNY Fredonia maybe twenty years ago and I'd like to read something to you that I wrote about that experience." In a voice loud and clear enough for everyone in the hall to hear, he replied, "Spare me."

I hated him for a few years after that, but not enough to overcome my love of his poetry and my gratitude for his example as a courageous rebel. By the time he died, years later, I had come to a kind of acceptance of the whole experience. I had come to realize that he was an old man that day at Brooklyn College and that maybe he already had some of the aches and pains that were the precursors to the cancer that would eventually kill him. Certainly, my appreciation of the entirety of the man had grown exponentially since that day, long and long before, when I'd first met him at SUNY Fredonia, that day he'd been so gracious to me.

Even our greatest heroes are imperfect human beings, just like the rest of us. Those two words – spare me – were like daggers to my young heart … but I'm a little older today, a little wiser. As much as I want to give my love and get it back from others, I must remember that, in some essential and irrevocable ways, each human being is a separate and private world unto himself. I must remember to rejoice when my world succeeds in uniting with another's, and not be overly surprised or stung when it does not.

Food Shapes

I'm not sure if I remember those little jars of Gerber's custard from when I was a baby or from when my high school buddy and I had the munchies and we'd make a quick run to Waldbaum's and buy half a dozen of them. It doesn't matter; I can still taste them, still return to my earliest experiences of them every time I bite into a pastry with even the remotest hint of their elemental flavor. Food shapes us. On Friday nights, my father's gefilte fish and my mother's chicken with *rayshuxs* (sweet gravy made with onions and ketchup) were a constant, and delicious to boot. But it wasn't just the food itself that left such a cherished and formative impression; it was the context. I remember, freezing winter nights, walking home from shule and stepping over the threshold, the warmth of the house, the glow of the *Shabbis* candles, the smells from the kitchen, my father making the blessings and cutting the *challah*, those first incredible bites assuaging a boyhood hunger that was deeper and more pleasant than any I've known since.

But if the *physical* hunger was deeper as a child, the overall appreciation of food and its prominent place in my life is much deeper today, and continues to grow. In my freshman year at SUNY Fredonia, there was this flower child named Bill who lived across the hall from me in the dorms. He was incredibly sweet and generous and he sometimes shared the brown rice/cheese/tofu dishes he'd create with his little plug-in toaster oven. I was beginning to experiment with vegetarianism at the time, but I hardly ever cooked and my staples were relatively tasteless salads and peanut butter sandwiches. Bill's healthful creations were little miracles to me; it was obvious that the way he ate was an essential part of who he was and I was drawn to him. One weekend, he invited me to go to Buffalo where Guru Maharaji was speaking. My mother thought I was going to end up joining some kind of cult, but I went anyway and had a great time. I remember a bunch of us crashed at someone's house, our sleeping bags spread out all over the floor. In the morning, I awoke to the most intoxicating smell. One of the hippies had cooked oatmeal for the entire troop, but this was not just the usual Quaker Oats; there were exotic spices, home-grown herbs, and who knows what else mixed into it. To this day, it was, by far, the best bowl of oatmeal I've ever eaten.

A few years later, I was walking down one of the main drags on the campus of SUNY Brockport and I noticed a guy standing up in a tree. He looked so natural and relaxed, he might have been waiting for a bus. His straight dark hair hung almost to his waist and I think we exchanged a few friendly words that day. By the end of the semester, we'd become good friends. One weekend, we were camping with a bunch of our schoolmates and I was amazed, the first morning, to see Noah serving pancakes in the middle of the woods!

He'd even brought maple syrup for us! I was beginning to understand that the taste of food wasn't limited to what went into my mouth and my stomach. It was also about the people who made the food, the people who ate it with you, where you were, where your head was at that moment. If smell is the strongest memory we possess, then the smell of food is exponential memory.

My father and mother both worked in the dining room of the Concord Hotel in upstate New York before they were married; it was there that they first started dating. One day, my father was passing through the kitchen after serving lunch. He was on his way out for a couple hours' break before he'd have to return to work dinner that night. He was almost at the door when a strange, sweet aroma pulled him back. He noticed a few of the Indian guys from the kitchen crew sitting over in the corner eating, so he walked over to say hi and find out what was giving off that incredible smell. They invited him to sit down and try it. My mom and dad were very soon hooked on each other and on Indian food. We had it regularly with them for years, growing up. Today, when I sit down to a meal in an Indian restaurant, I'm not only tasting the food; I'm tasting all those memories.

I guess you can take any one part of life and figure out a way to connect it to all the other parts. But, with food, it's different. With food, there's no effort. It's like breathing: I don't need to think about it; it just happens all by itself. From Gerber's custard to Bill's toaster-oven concoctions to the delicious soup my wife made for me yesterday, food has been nourishing me for sixty-four years.

In his essay, "The American Scholar," Emerson writes, "as the human body can be nourished on any food, though it were boiled grass and the broth of shoes, so the human mind can be fed by any knowledge." Now that's a nice analogy, and it's certainly true. But, to anyone who has read even a little more of Emerson than just that, it's quite clear he is *not* suggesting we settle for the lowest possible degree of nourishment; rather, he is implying the existence of a *hierarchy* of nourishment that is virtually boundless and subtly telling us, in his inimitable way, to reach higher, *much* higher, whether our intention is to feed our stomachs alone, or to include, as well, the minds and spirits that are magically, inextricably, linked to them.

Vision Quest

Toward the beginning of summer in 1992, a friend of mine showed me an ad he'd cut out of a newspaper and asked if I was interested in what they were offering. The ad was an invitation to take part in a "vision quest," a ten-day camping trip in the Adirondacks that would include immersion in both the substance and the spirit of several North American Indian rituals. I had always loved Indians as a kid and, over the years, had learned a little bit about what has come to be known as *the vision quest*: it was an excursion into the wilderness that the elders of a tribe organized and required of their youngsters; it was an important rite-of-passage in the life of a young Native American. I guess it was analogous to a Jewish boy's bar mitzvah, except that instead of just having the relatively light burden of learning a Torah portion and reciting it in front of your community, the Indian boy had to go into the forest, alone, and confront a series of mental, physical and spiritual challenges to prove his mettle. I told my friend I'd love to go.

Once we signed up, we received a very detailed list of what to bring, the most surprising line of which read: "ten pounds of fresh fruit and vegetables." We later found out there were fourteen participants and four leaders; that meant at least 180 pounds of fresh food! The leaders had hiked in to our site prior to the quest and, together, had hauled in *way* more than forty pounds; we needed every bit of it.

The primary leader, the guy who organized the whole thing, was a wonderful naturalist and teacher named Joseph. For our initial meeting spot, he had us park our cars a half mile or so down the road from where we'd be parking for the actual quest. He led us a short distance into the woods, where he stopped us to get organized and prepare for what was to come. We were told to get everything out of our packs and then reload them. This was not only to ensure that we had everything we needed, but also to distribute it all in such a way that the pack would be as balanced and secure as possible; we'd be hiking a long way, with a lot of weight, in the morning. Once we had our packs redone, he told us to put them on and follow him.

As we walked, Joseph pointed out that our feet were used to the smooth, level sidewalks of suburbia and that we needed to acclimate to the different ground here if we wanted to avoid accident and possible injury. He told us to stop walking and to close our eyes. He then had us take a few steps, but very slowly, concentrating on feeling the weight of the pack shifting with each step, the unevenness of the ground, the roots and the rocks and the crookedness of it all. We were encouraged to allow our feet to be our eyes for a time, to pay attention to the slight adjustments they instinctively made for the ground they now trod. This little exercise gave us our first impression of Joseph: we knew, without any doubt, we were in very good hands.

He had us set up our tents that first night right there, close to the road, so if anyone really needed anything he could always drive into town and get it. Once we hiked deep into the wilderness the next morning, that would no longer be an option.

The trail followed the north fork of the Bouquet River for several miles, and we had to cross it a couple times within the first hour, something much trickier with a heavy pack on your back. We were on state land, not far from the little town of Keene Valley, New York, and the surrounding mountains meant there was lots of water. The sights and sounds and smells were beyond beautiful and this helped alleviate the weight we carried. The trail had moved significantly away from the river by now, climbing gradually up a mountainside, a peaceful woods quiet replacing the percussion of the rapids. After what felt like a very long time, Joseph stopped by an upright boulder and explained, quite seriously, that this was Guardian Rock and that only those among us with the purest of intentions should pass it; the spirits of the land beyond were ready to embrace us and protect us, but only if our hearts were in the right place. If that statement sounds like horseshit to you, I'm sorry. For us, standing there at that moment in those woods, it rang perfectly real and true and each one of us touched Guardian Rock with reverence as he passed.

There really was a different feel to the land almost immediately upon passing that sacred boulder. The river had leveled off considerably and we were now more in a valley than on the side of a mountain. Sunlight reached us more consistently here and birdsong suddenly filled the air. After a couple miles or so, we reached the site our guides had so masterfully prepared. There was a huge tepee-like structure with a fire pit underneath and logs all around. The hole at the top allowed smoke to escape and we were able to sit under there even in a heavy rain and enjoy our circle.

We all spread out within twenty or thirty yards of our communal teepee and found level ground for our tents. Cooking and cleaning chores were shared and we created some amazing meals together. Two hand-carved forked sticks had been set up on either side of the fire, with a thick wire running between them from which we could hang a big pot. For breakfast the first day, we had hot oatmeal with freeze-dried strawberries stirred in; it was the first time I'd ever eaten strawberries that way and they were a surprise luxury; food always tastes better in the woods, but the gourmet meals we whipped up would have been delicious anywhere. Early every morning, like clockwork, Hubbs, my favorite of the four leaders after Joseph, would let out a barbaric yawp just before slapping the water with a perfect racing dive. He was an unusual guy, very quiet, but when he spoke, it was clear he chose his words carefully and you wanted to listen. A beautiful harmony and simplicity began to evolve among us; Joseph's spirit was one of the primary reasons for this: he was such a relaxed, loving man, but he was also very strong and decisive. Everything he said and everything he did exemplified health and balance; it was the same with Hubbs. To live with such wholesome, light-filled men, even for just a few days, was contagious.

Around halfway through our time in the woods together, we were split up into two work crews to prepare the sweat lodge. My crew spent hours gathering dead branches and cutting them up for firewood. The other crew constructed the actual lodge and set up the two pits needed to make it all work, one for fire and the other for steam. That night, we got a huge blaze going. A fireman had been appointed to ensure continuous heat. Earlier, while we were out collecting wood, he had placed several good-sized rocks in the fire pit, and now, whenever we needed a fresh burst of steam, he would open up the flap of the lodge and, using a big shovel I'd not noticed before, retrieve one of the glowing stones and roll it right into the second pit the crew had dug in the center of the lodge. He would then pour ice-cold water from the stream onto the rock and a cloud of hot steam would immediately fill the lodge. Here we were, in the middle of the woods on a cold night, and yet we were dripping wet with sweat! After a few hours of singing and drumming and screaming, we all plunged into the stream, wearing nothing but moonlight. We felt clean to the bone … nay, to the *soul*.

The next morning, we all went off on our own for three days of solitude and meditation. Joseph provided us all with air horns in case there was an emergency and someone needed help. Some of us fasted during these days. I didn't, but I ate very light and very well. I had pitched my tent on a long and narrow island in the middle of the river just upstream from where it forked; a bit further upstream, the two forks blended again. The first time I went for a swim, I realized that climbing back up and into the tent without bringing in mud and sand from my feet would be impossible. I decided to make myself a little walkway. There were plenty of stones around, so I took my time finding six or seven flat ones that would serve as steps. The walkway worked like a charm. Years later, when I had a deck and shower built in my suburban backyard, I insisted on a similar design to keep my feet clean; I didn't want any sand or gravel or dirt sticking to them once I was done showering.

After setting everything up, I went for a little swim and then, before going in the tent, decided to try hiking around a little bit wearing just my birthday suit. Nobody was around; Walking Owl, my nearest neighbor, was at least a hundred yards upstream. The trees and the slant of the land there prevented us from seeing each other and the whitewater drowned out all other sounds.

I started walking, and my non-woods brain immediately started flashing yellow lights, warning me to stop, to beware: you'll step on something sharp; you'll get stung on your bare ass, or even worse! But something in the peace of that time and place, or maybe the peace of Joseph and Hubbs that had already rubbed off on me a little bit by then – whatever it was – convinced to keep walking. The sun soon dried me, and I found a big rock to climb up on and sit still. My lesser brain started worrying again: surely now, when I'm not moving at all, some giant bee will find my cock and go to town. But I listened to the birds, took some deep belly-breaths, and managed to fight off the fear, to replace it with a trust that everything around me was benign. I sat on that rock, cross-legged, and breathed in the woods air of that place for at least a half hour. Not so much as a mosquito came near me.

I could go on for ten pages about the ten days, but let me just leave you with this: everything we did seamlessly flowed into everything else; there was a Wholeness to those ten days in the woods that I have seldom, if ever, experienced again: we cooked together, we ate together, we worked together, we cried together. We shared each other's joy and we shared each other's pain. Hubbs had reminded us to eat each meal as though it were our last and Joseph had reminded us to embrace the unknown, not to run from it. We had gone our individual ways during the solitary time, but then we united once again, in our circle, around our fire, and listened carefully to each other's stories.

When we hiked back out of those woods, we were changed men. Each one of us had achieved a little more solidity in his life, felt a bit more certain of the direction he would now pursue. There was a kind of magic to it all, but not a hocus-pocus kind of magic; rather, the kind of magic we felt that first time we passed Guardian Rock. There is a power in the wilderness that is different from the power in the city. Man's creations are admirable, but God's creations are miraculous. To be immersed in them is, in some mysterious way, to share in their power, to imbibe a divine nectar, like a flower drinking sunshine. We all came away nourished by those ten days, and, unbelievable as this may be, it is nourishment that is somehow still with me, still feeding me, even all these twenty-eight years later.

Maintaining Balance

In Japan, there is an expression "mizu no kokoro" or "mind like water." It's a good way to be. I would say it's a good way to think, but that would be missing the point. It's about being so open, so yielding and receptive to what's happening right now, that what we call thinking is not really taking place; it's more of a spontaneous response to whatever life presents, moment by moment. I'm not very good at this, but I'm trying to learn.

One thing I *do* know is that it has everything to do with keeping one's balance, regardless of the twists and turns we encounter. Just as all the creatures within the natural world perform their tasks within very delicate and balanced ecosystems, so too, our own bodies are ecosystems whose myriad, interconnected parts we can either nourish or pollute. This is an obvious truth. But nothing is obvious when it comes to our interactions with those *outside* of our bodies, with people. How do we decide where to draw the line with *them* between what is enough and what is too much, between what would be considered reasonable and what would be considered fanatical? Well, that all depends on who is doing the considering. If you say, "most people," that really doesn't help much, because "most people" is another way of saying "common sense" and Emerson reminds us that sometimes what is needed is precisely *un*common sense: not what *most* people think; rather, what you, *yourself,* think in those crucial moments when you're brave enough to take the road less traveled, when you're free enough to be yourself instead of someone else's shadow. This morning, it feels like I have challenges closing in on me from every side and I don't know which way to turn: my younger son is at the height of his teenage angst, my wife is upset with me because I keep putting things down on the dining room table, even my dog is a problem this morning; he has an upset stomach.

But what's really pushing me over the edge is the situation with my mother. She just turned ninety-two and my brother Steve approached me a couple weeks ago with the idea of moving her back into his house instead of her having to continue shelling out four thousand a month at The Nautilus. I was hesitant to have her move back in with him because, the last time Mom lived at his house, a year and a half ago, Steve had specifically called to tell me the situation was getting dangerous; he had said she was often completely alone and his long stairway was an accident waiting to happen. I had completely agreed with him and quickly facilitated the move into The Nautilus.

Even though I was very reluctant to have her move back in with him now, I wanted to be supportive and so I agreed; all I asked in return was that he set her up *downstairs* this time. I tried to enlist my sister Pamela as an ally in this prudent qualification, but to no avail. Both she and Steve insisted Mom was doing fine and told me I shouldn't worry about something that may never happen. My mind, on the other hand, kept looking to the future, imagining various scenarios, hearing the statistics of seniors who fall and never return from the hospital. I thought I was being perfectly reasonable, especially since *Steve* was the one who'd initiated moving her out because of his stairway: if that had been one of his primary reasons for moving her out back then, what's going to be any different now? If anything, Mom is older and even *more* frail; a fall would be even *more* likely!

I don't want to be in conflict with anyone; I'm just trying to play the percentages, to keep my mom as safe as she can possibly be. There's a balance to everything, and one of the more important ones is probably the balance between listening to what others have to say and listening to yourself. When these two contradict, as they invariably will, perhaps we find ourselves in the kind of stalemate that requires *mizo no kokoro*, mind like water. As I said earlier, I'm not very good at that kind of non-thinking, but I'm trying. Maybe I should *not* try. I started thinking about all this a couple days ago when I happened to be flipping through an old journal of mine and came across the following passage I'd copied from an Alan Watts paperback:

An excellent example of sensitivity to the moment is found in the application of Zen to kendo (swordsmanship). No amount of drilled-in reflexes or rules can prepare the swordsman for the infinity of different attacks which he may have to face, especially when confronted with more than one opponent. He is taught, therefore, never to make any specific preparation for attack nor to expect it from any particular direction. Otherwise, to meet an unusual attack, he will have to retreat from one stance before being able to adopt another. He must be able to spring immediately from a relaxed center of rest to the direction required. This relaxed openness of sensitivity in every direction is precisely "kuan," or, as it more commonly called in Zen, "mushin," which is to say, "no mind," no strain of the mind to watch for a particular result.

I'm hoping that I can somehow apply what Watts had to say here to everything I do, including my interactions with family. It ain't going to be easy, but practice helps. Already, I feel myself inhabiting a more "relaxed center of rest" than I was this just morning. I guess the more I see that what ends up happening is completely different from what I expected, the easier it will be for me to simply be more present, more "able to spring immediately" into whatever new direction is required. I'm not quite there yet, but I'm making progress.

Scaling the Heights

Every morning, especially lately, I get up and check the list I've prepared for what I must do that particular day; the list is always incomplete, but I know I have the rest of my life to add to it and work on it … and I fully accept that my inbox will keep filling up no matter how much progress I think I'm making. In fact, that's probably what this is really about: progress. Not so much the *number* of things that get done, but the relative *grace* I'm able to maintain while doing them. Just last night, I didn't act very gracefully. But I got up today determined to be better. There is always some new measurement to consider, some slight adjustment to make, some subtle realignment that will grease the wheels of my life and make it run better. You've probably heard of the serenity prayer: "God grant me the serenity to accept the things I cannot change; the courage to change the things I can; and the wisdom to know the difference." Maybe my biggest problem is that last part – knowing the difference between what *is* my business and what *isn't*. Still, no matter how many mistakes I make, I know that, in the long arc of my life, I *am* making *some* progress. Hopefully, even this will be the year that will drown out all my muskrats; or, if not all of them, at least the ones that most impede my progress.

The list I generate each day is comprised of those things that, once completed, will put a bit more order into my current world. Over time, if I'm consistent, all these seemingly trivial things can add up and allow me to feel a bit better about myself, maybe even enough to make a bigger difference this year than I did in the last; can't be lazy. The give-away bag is full and needs to be dropped off at the Good Will box on National Blvd. It's going to rain today so the attic windows must be closed. The writing class at The Nautilus resumes at eleven o' clock this morning; there are handouts to prepare. Forgot a few items at Trader Joe's yesterday; must drive over there soon. Got to stop leaving my clothes on the dining room chair, show Liza more love. Need to stop neglecting my sit ups; they're the best way to keep my back from going out again.

Life is movement and growth. There is no holding it back. And if you're not moving and growing with it, you can very quickly get left in the dust. But over and above all of these things is the body itself. It's hard to balance everything outside of ourselves and still pay sufficient attention to our own bodies; but that's exactly what we must do if we truly wish to function at maximum efficiency, joy, and grace. I remember Thoreau writing that we should guard against acquisitions so that we can better concentrate on taking care of what we already have: *How many a poor immortal soul have I met well-nigh crushed and smothered under its load, creeping down the road of life, pushing before it a barn seventy-five feet by forty, its Augean stables never cleansed, and one hundred acres of land, tillage, mowing, pasture, and wood-lot. The portionless, who struggle with no such unnecessary inherited encumbrances, find it labor enough to subdue and cultivate a few cubic feet of flesh.*

I have never taken that to mean that we should strive to be completely "portionless," but we can certainly embrace a good idea without taking it to an extreme. Every morsel we put into our mouths and every drop of exercise we engage in are tiny weights on the scales of each day. We can be conscious of this without being fanatical. No matter what level of self-care we practice, there is no escaping the fact that we are in these bodies for now and they are the machines with which we live the physical parts of our existence. The great sages of the world have always spoken of mind, body and spirit as being inseparable and interdependent. I feel the truth of this when I have had just one cookie too many; but I also feel the truth of this when I have treated myself well for a few days and am back on the path of self-integration instead of self-destruction. The choices seem so clear then; they get murkier when I'm weak.

The Bible tells us we are created in God's image. If this is so, and I believe that it is, then it's perfectly natural for us to be confident, to be creative, to assert our power and make a positive contribution to the world. Moses, on the other hand, the great leader who led the ancient Israelites from the bondage of Egypt to the Promised Land of Israel, was said to be the humblest man that ever lived. So which is it? Should we move forward with confidence or with humility? I guess this is where the need for balance comes in: instead of choosing one or the other, we must aspire to maintain that ever-shifting point between two necessary opposites, that magical spot between the ever-shifting swirls of yin and yang. It ain't easy, but the alternative is a crippling self-shame that can snowball over time. We don't need to put in a *perfect* day, but when we put in a good one, we *know* it, our head fits more snugly into the pillow at night, our sleep comes more easily, and our dreams yield a bone-deep peace that is unknown to those who go to bed with a bad conscience.

This past Sunday was Father's Day. Something came up that wasn't on my list but found its way into my life anyway. I had noticed a lot of trash while walking the dog and decided to go back out with a big bag and gather it all up. Several people saw me doing it. I imagined what they might have been thinking, but the most important part of the experience was what *I* was thinking. Had I been a teacher watching one of my students do this job, I would have put a gold star on his forehead. I guess, in some mysterious way, I am both the teacher of that student and the student himself. The star feels good just above and between my eyes. My telling you about all this doesn't diminish it in the least for me. I didn't take the action to get credit for it; what I did was its own reward. Even though it's relatively trivial and only took thirty minutes or so, it will forever be in my memory now, forever a part, however minutely, of the fabric of my life, forever helping me to balance my warring scales.

A listing, a balancing, an accounting … it doesn't matter much what you call it; it matters that you *do* it. Another way to say it could be "a measuring." So much of our lives involves measuring of one kind or another. Even something as seemingly insignificant as our fingernails can become a problem if they're too long or too short. Just today, my wife told me our dog was licking his paw and she thought there might be something going on there. Sure enough, when I put my glasses on and got a good look, I saw she was right: one of his nails was cracked and hanging; if I didn't take care of it right away, it might pull up into his cuticle and really cause a problem. I managed to muzzle him with the cloth belt from my bathrobe and clipped the hanging part off fairly easily. But that's just one example of thousands. There's a "too little" and a "too much" to just about everything we encounter in this life. And the progress I mentioned earlier is primarily, I think, about finding that sweet spot between them, the place where we feel good about the contribution we're making, the place where we know, at least for a moment, that our presence, our behavior, is contributing to *solving* the problem rather than causing it.

There's so much conflict in the world right now. How can we voice a divergent opinion without offending anyone? It's hard not to say too much or too little. The people I admire the most are those who allow their actions to speak for them; people get their message from the way they live their lives. I start each day before sunrise on the beach with the dog. There's usually nobody out at that early hour and it's easier to keep quiet. While running along the shore, snatches of the day's list occur to me momentarily and then go out with the tide. It is my mind, especially, that needs constant balancing: I want to remember what I wish to get done today, but I don't want to think about it so much that I'm missing the present before me. The chimney guy is coming on Tuesday; I need to have fire bricks ready for him. Should I get an extra tent so Dave doesn't have to lug his big one all the way to our campsite? How strict should I be with my nineteen-year-old who's acting out? Where do I draw the line? Where is the point of balance?

I want to deal with all of these things as directly and mindfully as possible, even if they're difficult; putting them off accomplishes nothing. Imagine you have a huge mound of snow that must be moved from point A to point B; it all seems overwhelming until you begin the work. And then, immediately, you feel better, each shovelful lightening the burden. A single white gull glides by against a backdrop of orange-tinged clouds, gently breaking my stream of thought; muffled explosions of waves keep hitting the beach, a calming music that encourages me to take a couple deep belly breaths, start my day from a more centered place. My list is now a gift instead of a chore. A feeling of great freedom comes to me when I remember that the way I *think* about things can be adjusted too, can be recalibrated every time I learn some better way to care of myself, my loved ones, or our planet.

There are so many ways we can nurture ourselves and others, so many little projects we can put on our lists and then incrementally bring to fruition; but we must be ever vigilant, fully awake to our power and our choices, to the small steps we can take to make this world a little better at the end of the day than it was at the beginning. *A man's reach should exceed his grasp, or what's a heaven for?* Damn right! So why do I keep neglecting to do those sit ups? I need to be more awake.

We need to keep reaching, no matter how much we think we've already accomplished. When we do that, and we do it *consistently*, the accounting we take of ourselves at the end of the day will allow for a sweeter sleep than any we've ever had … and the accounting that is taken *of us* at the end of our bodies will result in the soul's elevation to an even greater sphere of opportunity and growth than the one we're moving through now.

Love Your Neighbor as You Love Yourself

A few weeks ago, the following famous words from the Book of Leviticus were heard in temples throughout the world. The time of year for this particular portion to be part of the weekly Torah reading had arrived again: *You shall neither take revenge from nor bear a grudge against the members of your people; you shall love your neighbor as yourself. I am the Lord.* Even the most devout Jews question how one could possibly "love your neighbor as you love yourself." However, a *Chabad* rabbi recently told a true story by way of offering some insight into how this could actually be achieved … the state of mind one must possess in order to fulfill this most difficult but crucial mitzvah. This is that true story:

One day, a young girl named Sarah woke up in her home in Israel and was startled to discover she could no longer speak normally; she suddenly had such a terrible stutter that she could not get through a single sentence without faltering. She could hardly say her own name without stuttering. Sarah's parents were quite well off and they took her to the best doctors and specialists, but none of them could do anything. They said they had seen this before, though rarely, and that this particular condition sometimes arises spontaneously and will sometimes disappear spontaneously; but they could offer no definitive therapies or predictions. Fortunately, Sarah loved school and continued to enjoy her studies. Socially, however, things got very difficult for her. Her friends began to feel uncomfortable and gradually abandoned her. Her love of learning was the one bright spot in her life during the next few years. She continued to excel in her classes and graduated toward the top of her high school class. In college, her life continued in a similar fashion: academically, things were great; but, socially, she was not doing very well. When she graduated college and started going out on job interviews, she experienced a new kind of rejection: after she spoke just a few words, the interviewer would invariably cut short the meeting and thank her for coming in. For years now, through all her difficulties, Sarah had always maintained her confidence and positive attitude. But this felt like the straw that would break her back. She was seriously considering giving up and resigning herself to a life far less than the one she'd always dreamed for herself. But then something happened.

A very successful businessman, Yigal, the owner of a large company, woke up one morning and decided he would sit in on the interview scheduled for that day. He usually let his subordinates handle all the interviews, but for some mysterious reason he felt compelled to participate in this one. Sarah arrived at Yigal's company early that day and she was soon shown into a conference room in which three men sat at a table waiting to ask her questions. Unlike all her previous interviews, in this one, she was *not* shown the door after speaking just a few words. The first two men questioned her and patiently listened as she stuttered through her answers. Then Yigal asked if she could return the next day at 9 am. Sarah replied, "Of course," and Yigal said he'd see her tomorrow. As she returned to the outer office where she'd first come in, she overheard Yigal's voice on the intercom instructing his secretary to "have everything ready for Sarah to begin working tomorrow."

Sure enough, Sarah was hired and, after a relatively short period of time, became an invaluable asset to the company. She loved her job and all her coworkers and everyone there loved her too. It was as though a dark cloud had been lifted from her life. She soon met a wonderful young man and was married. Things could not have been better. One day, an invitation arrived in the mail. It was from Yigal. His son was about to become a Bar-Mitzvah and he wanted Sarah to attend the ceremony and celebratory meal. She immediately ran out to purchase a very special present. Then, she told her husband she wanted to drive over to Yigal's house and deliver the present personally. She didn't want her present to be just one among many. She wanted to go out of her way to show Yigal how much she appreciated all he had done for her. His hiring her that day almost three years before had transformed her life. Her husband was totally supportive and agreed they should drive over immediately.

Sarah rang Yigal's bell and he opened the door with a big smile on his face. "Sarah!" he said. "I wasn't expecting to see you until Saturday! To what do I owe this most pleasant surprise?" Sarah explained that she simply wanted to convey her deep appreciation for all his kindness from the moment they first met until the moment she'd received the invitation that morning. If not for his kindness and patience that day of her interview, she had no idea what her life would be like now; certainly nothing nearly as good. She thanked him profusely and he received all her words with sincere humility and appreciation. They exchanged some pleasantries and Sarah was about to leave, but then she stopped and asked if she could ask him about something that had been on her mind a very long time. "Of course," Yigal replied. "Why did you hire me?" she asked him. "Why were you so incredibly patient and tolerant with me that day three years ago at the interview? Everyone else had gotten rid of me before I could speak a second sentence. Why were you so kind to me?"

Yigal's smiling face turned serious and he began to explain: "That morning of your interview, I don't know what made me think of sitting in; I had never done that before. When I first heard you speak, I was about to get up and leave the room, thinking my business required someone who could speak fluidly, with complete grace; I was concerned about how your speech might turn away clients. But then I thought of my son, and that gave me pause. Five years ago, he woke up to find he had a stutter as severe as yours. We brought him to all the experts, but no one could do anything for him. What stopped me from prematurely rejecting you that morning was the thought that, one day, my son would be a young man going out on job interviews. I was struck with the realization that I must treat you exactly the way I would want some prospective employer out there in the world to treat my son. Thankfully, his stuttering vanished last year as mysteriously as it had arrived. Tomorrow, you will hear him deliver his Bar-Mitzvah speech in a clear, mellifluous voice. I wish I could tell you that my kindness and tolerance that day of the interview came naturally to me, but that would not be true. It was only the consciousness of my own son's condition at that time that enabled me to treat you the way I did. I can only hope that, as I get older, my ability to love my neighbor as I love myself will become an ingrained habit instead of a fleeting moment of inspiration."

Special thanks to Rabbi Eli Goodman & Rabbi Chilik Weinfeld

Dream Time Arising

My earliest memory is of a place we called the Peewee Lot. Is was a big vacant lot down the block from our apartment building on Sterling Street in Brooklyn. We called it the Peewee Lot because we invariably took a leak in there while playing combat or hide and seek or whatever it was we happened to be playing that particular day. The lot was strewn with pieces of lumber and other refuse the adult people had dumped there. But it was great because, for us, these were things we could hide behind – probably the only place we had any true privacy from everyone, including our parents. The act of peeing in public without being seen by anyone was emblematic of the freedom we felt there; the Peewee Lot was ours alone. Once we'd had our fill of independence, we'd head back to the playground where mom was patiently waiting. Before long, the beautiful notes of the Mr. Softee ice cream truck could be heard approaching and mom would flip us each a quarter. Back then, that was all you needed for a small cone with sprinkles. This was probably 1960 or 61 and I was around four or five.

Shortly after that, we moved into the main level of a two-family house in Manhattan Beach. I always assumed the people who lived downstairs were the owners; but now that I think about it, they may have been just tenants too, like us. The house was on Irwin Street, a nice tree-lined block running between the bay and the ocean. The Pullmans were our neighbors and, boy, were they rich! The kid my age had a playroom that was so big, you could ride a bicycle in it! His dad had a big, black antique car he'd take out only on Sundays and special occasions. We used to visit mom's sisters, Essie and Ruthie, often during these years. They lived very close to each other, just across the footbridge that led to Sheepshead Bay. Aunt Ruthie's apartment building had a big outdoor pool and, even though we swam at the beach every summer, it was still a treat to get into a pool once in a while; it made us feel as though we'd "moved on up to the east side." Aunt Essie's building had this really neat basement. In the summer, she'd give us some change to get a container of milk from the machine down there; it was always nice and cool compared to anything street level or above. But the icing on the cake was this huge storage room we'd discovered, just off the main corridor, where all the tenants kept their bicycles, strollers, scooters and toy cars. We'd have a ball in there for hours, riding around on other kids' stuff.

In 1963, we moved to Long Beach and the little bit of knowledge we'd acquired about sand and surf blossomed into a way of life. Kids who grow up in a beach town have a natural playground waiting for them at the end of every block. We still have parents and teachers and police to keep us in line, but, somehow, we're able to breathe a little bit easier. There's something about all that space and all that bracing sea air that is very freeing. Everyone needs that – especially kids. I was now in the third grade, and, although still in yeshiva, I started noticing girls in a new way. Mysterious and elemental processes were evolving within me, and I'm quite certain that my taste in women began to form even then, no matter how primitive and naïve these beginnings may have been. But there were other parts to growing up that weren't so much fun. One day, I was playing basketball with my cousins who had yarmulkes on their heads; their dad is my Uncle Natie, a Rabbi. A bunch of Black kids approached and started hassling us for no reason other than the fact that they had seen the yarmulkes and they smelled blood. One of them, a really skinny kid, suddenly punched me right in the face. I could've probably destroyed him, he was so thin, but instinctively knew not to hit back; we were the only white kids in the entire playground and the place was packed. He popped me a couple more times, all on the same side of my face, but we were able to leave soon afterwards without further incident. To this day, I still feel a little ashamed for not fighting back, but most of me believes I did the right thing. There's a line in a film that goes something like this: "The first man to raise his fist is the man who has run out of ideas." I only ran out of ideas twice in my entire life – once in elementary school and once in eighth grade. I guess not getting *myself* beat up was always more important to me than any satisfaction I might get from beating up someone *else*; Of course, my small size had everything to do with my calculus at the time … and still does.

I left yeshiva after ninth grade and entered the unsheltered environs of Long Beach High School. Our many summers in Monticello had allowed me to mix with all kinds of kids, but that was just a couple months a year. Now, for the first time, I was completely immersed within the secular world and it was a shock to my relatively pampered system. I remember, my very first week in the building, we were sitting on one of those wide benches they had in the Commons when this huge guy with a strangely shaped head walks by. "Who's the guy with the square head?" I asked in something between a whisper and my normal voice. My brother and his friends immediately, *dramatically*, shushed me. "Are you crazy?" they asked. "That's Anson Duncan, the toughest guy in the West End! He'll kill you quick as look at you!" They weren't kidding; we heard Duncan was arrested for murder just a few years out of high school. But most of the shocks I received in this new wide world opening up to me were of the good variety. Fortunately, although I was exposed to all kinds of temptations, all kinds of opportunities for instant gratification, I usually resisted being pulled more than I thought was enough. I certainly experimented here and there – I'm not a machine, after all – but I didn't really undergo any major transformation; on the contrary, as I look back on it now, I can see that my time in high school, though certainly indelible, was still just one chapter among many, just one more of the varied spheres of influence that had been presenting themselves to me, and would continue to present themselves to me, like so many dishes at a smorgasbord, as my young self was finding his way.

For the most part, I took what I thought was useful and left the rest behind. At that point, what I considered most useful was playing basketball and getting high, not studying; as a result, I had to take what I could get when it came time for college. When a guidance counselor wrote down the names of four schools that might accept me despite my paltry average, I put all four of them on a single application to save my parents money. SUNY Fredonia, way out on the western edge of the state and known for its music department, opened its doors to me and off I gratefully went. That was the first year I'd ever lived on my own, but I still somehow managed to maintain some kind of balance between work and play. I had seen my father working two jobs for too long to betray his trust in me or waste his hard-earned money. High school was one thing; this was something else entirely. I guess part of growing up means beginning to decide what kind of a person you want to be and being willing to do the work necessary to get there; of course, this entails far more than just school work. Dad had done a little creative bartering with some radio guy and managed to get me a brand-new Atala racing bike just before I left home. I pedaled all over Erie County on that bike. This was a new kind of freedom. I would hold off buying a car for years, until I actually needed one to get to work; little by little, I was learning the advantages of self-discipline. I think I'd first read Thoreau's *Walden* in high school, but now I was beginning to embrace his idea that "a man is rich in proportion to the things he can do without." Joe DeVeaux and I often stayed up past midnight singing old Dylan tunes. Big Smile Bill, across the hall, beautifully exemplified the benefits of vegetarianism and Eastern philosophies. I had been leaning toward these things for years, tinkering with them, but now I was soaking them up like a hungry sponge.

Toward the end of second semester, Bobby called me up one night and asked if I'd like to go to Israel with him for a year. Mom and dad had said they'd chip in half the air fare and that's all it would cost! Working on a kibbutz is a wonderful place for a penniless college student; you're made to feel very welcome there as long as you're not some mooch who expects to live off other people's sweat. Kibbutzniks work hard and they respect people who pull their own weight. If this is the way Communism started out, I thought, it's a damn shame people screwed it up; it sure works beautifully when it's done right, though. We worked for seven months at Kibbutz Merchavia, once the home of Golda Meir. After that, I moved to Kibbutz Nir David, a place contiguous with a beautiful park we'd visited on an outing some months before. I had watched everyone swimming in its spring-fed river that day, but couldn't go in with the cast still on my ankle from a bad landing in a basketball game. But I never forgot the look of that turquoise water, the waterfalls, the cave you could swim into and disappear. Bobby had a private room with air conditioning and a refrigerator and decided to stay put in Merchavia. My gut told me to move, and it's a good thing I listened. Almost every evening, at sunset, I would take the short hike upstream to the park and skinny-dip, colorful kingfishers crossing the twilit sky the only witnesses. It was a dream time for me, like so many other hours in this blessed life.

When I got back home, I drifted around for two-and-a-half years, taking odd jobs, not really sure what I wanted to do "for a living." My good buddy Dave had been inviting me to accompany him to his brother Bill's place in Jamaica practically since we met and this time I quickly accepted. Bill had married Rose, a Jamaican lady, years before, and Dave had flown there almost every summer since to be with them. We drove down to Coconut Grove in Karen Goldfinger's mother's car and stayed in her sister's house for New Year's Eve, 1977. It turns out Karen's sister was married to Billy Crystal! That night, we watched Billy on *The Tonight Show* on his own TV in his own house! I was hoping to get something going with Karen, but that never materialized. On January 2nd, Dave and I flew to Montego Bay and hitched a ride from the airport to his brother's little fishing village. From the moment the truck pulled away from the airport, and for the entire fifty kilometers to Green Island, all you smelled was flowers! It was unbelievable. Dave and I camped on his brother's land and cooked our meals on an open campfire. We swam in the pristine ocean every day and enjoyed a hot shower and a sumptuous home-cooked dinner every Sunday at Bill and Rose's. We ate big bowls of fish tea, drank little bottles of Red Stripe beer, and lived to the constant, relaxing beats of Rasta and Reggae. This was another dream time.

Back in The States, I thought about becoming a forest ranger and, the year after that, a phys. ed. teacher. I figured getting paid to hike around the woods or play ball would be a good deal, but the math and science courses required for these professions scared me away; back then, I would simply quit when things got tough. But running the NYC Marathon helped put an end to that. People always *say* you can accomplish anything you put your mind to, but the only way you can really *believe* that is by proving it to yourself. That 26.2-mile run in 1988 was certainly a good start for me. I'm still proving important things to myself, but it's more relaxed now; I'm in less of a hurry. "All we have is time," I heard myself telling my son yesterday. I returned to school, still not sure what I wanted to do, but kept taking classes I *liked* … no matter what they did for my resumé. Somebody told me to make sure I sign up for a Bill Heyen class, so I did. Bill became a mentor and friend and has had a huge impact on me. I stayed in sleepy little Brockport for four-and-a-half years, earning two degrees in English but, way more importantly, learning how to fine-tune this body, mind, and spirit we're all made up of … learning how to find the balance that brings greater health and joy and peace.

I started pursuing another degree at The Jewish Theological Seminary of America, then got tired of sharing a bathroom with three other guys, never having my own place, and never having any money, so I answered an ad reading, "Wanted: 300 teachers." A Mr. Rufus Thomas handed me a piece of paper with "Wingate High School" written on it. I took the subway from Manhattan to Brooklyn, then walked the few remaining blocks to what they called "the banjo school" because of its architecture. Although the inner-city was far from an optimal environment for teaching, I did meet my wife, Liza, there, and it was she who convinced me to leave when a stray bullet actually went through one of the school's windows. This was but the first of many good things she would convince me to do. I wrote to every district on Long Island and was lucky to land in Great Neck.

Eleven-and-a-half years at Wingate, twenty-one at Great Neck South, a beautiful wife, two strong sons, a great dog … I'm a very lucky man. How is it that my heart continues to pump blood day after day? How is it that my lungs keep inflating and deflating? Did I really camp in France and Italy those two summers? Did I really sing the High Holiday prayers as a cantor in Aruba? Did I really hike up a mountain to a tavern that day in the Swiss Alps? Did my sons and I really swim with dolphins off Grand Bahama Island? I look out the window here at school where I sub now a couple days a week, and my wonder continues … where does the leaves' golden color come from? What more can I learn of the Designer who formed the eagle's wing? I still don't have the answers to all my questions, not even close, but I feel certain every step of my journey was necessary to get me where I am today. There are no wasted motions. Every single lesson, every easy one and every hard one, was needed to bring me to this exact intersection of time and space. Be with me now, here, in this moment. Take a deep breath. Is it not true that the whole shebang is One Great Ecosystem in which we must play our small but indispensable parts … and for so short a time? Then let us resolve to do what we can to *sweeten* the ride, to ease the way a bit for ourselves and for our fellow travelers. *All your life, you were only waiting for this moment to arise.* Those Liverpool lads sure got that right. Think of the times you have lived, the times to come. Now move toward them with greater purpose, greater resolve. Are we dreaming all this or is it real?

Yes.

Finding the Sweet Spot

When you get on a scale at the doctor's office, they slide that big black weight into its slot and then fiddle with the little weight until there's a balance and a proper reading can be attained. This is something like what we do all the time: problems come up; situations develop. We need to figure out a way to somehow keep it all together, make it all work out … but there's no perfect weight at our fingertips to slide over, nothing to lock us into attaining what we desire or what we think we need. Instead, we must choose an *approximate* path to pursue, slide ourselves in that direction, and then fiddle with whatever little weights, whatever little choices, are within our reach, move them back and forth, test them, to the best of our ability, with our speech and our actions and our spirit, until we come to some kind of balance, some kind of equilibrium, some kind or peace. This is the calculation of life. In the animal world, it often comes down to predator versus prey; in our world, it's us against ourselves.

What I mean is, the outside forces are forever unpredictable. We will never have control over the people, places and things we encounter each day. We will never know whether the pitch hurtling toward us will be a fastball or a curve. And so it is up to us alone to adjust, to be ready for anything, to alter our stance or our swing for maximum performance regardless of the circumstances under which we are playing. The Boy Scouts taught us this when we were kids, their motto proudly displayed on our green uniforms: "Be Prepared."

But how do you prepare for those robotic voices on the telephone forever instructing you to "press 1" when all you want to do is talk to a real human being and ask one simple question? How do you prepare for relatives surprising you with behavior that resembles exactly the kind of thing Superman encountered whenever he visited the Bizarro World? People can be so thoughtless, so selfish, so ignorant! Why would someone throw a bag trash out the window of their moving car instead of waiting for a proper receptacle? I'm not venting here. I'm simply trying to steel myself for what's coming; apparently, my Boy Scouts training is far from sufficient.

The first rule of lifeguarding is probably what I most need to remember in order to better deal with this challenging, often frustrating part of life: keep *yourself* safe. If someone you're attempting to save starts panicking and taking you down, you need to get the hell away and save yourself first. It's like that instruction they give you on an airplane: put your *own* oxygen mask on before helping your child. The idea in both cases is that, if you're dead, you're not going to be of much use to anyone else. This is Selfishness with a capital

"S." In an analogous way, I'm reminded of that line in *The Old Man and the Sea* when Santiago thanks the boy for the bait. Hemingway writes: *He did not remember when he had attained humility, but he knew that he had attained it and he knew it carried no loss of true pride.* True pride as opposed to false pride; pride with a capital "P."

If you feel good about yourself, there's no need to put others down; in fact, you see them as your equals even if they're much younger and much less experienced. When you *don't* feel good about yourself, however, then you need to rely on a false kind of pride, on the misguided idea that you're better than someone else simply because you're older and it is therefore proper that they subordinate themselves before you. Santiago thanked the boy because he genuinely *appreciated* what the boy was doing for him; he was not so arrogant as to expect it. He had the kind of pride in himself that did not require the putting down of others.

Saving yourself in order to be better able to save others is a *good* kind of Selfishness. It is not the kind of selfishness that is practiced merely for the self; it is the kind of Selfishness that builds true pride and so leads to greater connection with our neighbors, greater community. It is the kind of Selfishness that allows us to appreciate others and to let them know it. It is the kind of Selfishness that allows us to feel fulfilled enough to *share* our wealth and our love and our energy instead of hoarding it. We need more of that kind of Selfishness in this world.

Stopped at the optometrist's today to get my reading glasses adjusted. Just before he was done with me, the technician got a phone call and wandered into the back of the store to retrieve some files for the person on the line. I started thinking, "Why the hell is this person on the phone getting taken care of when I'm right here? Shouldn't *he* be the one made to wait instead of me? I started calculating how unjust this was, went into a judgment mode that bit into my serenity. But I said nothing. A little smoke may have been issuing from my ears, but I don't think it was visible to anyone. My rising temperature sure was apparent to me, however. After only a minute or so, the technician returned, finished adjusting my glasses, and left me to consider how I had conducted myself in those few seconds, the toxicity I had so carelessly contributed to my inner world. If I gradually master these little annoyances, will that strengthen the muscle I need for the big ones? Will it enable me to strike a balance on these forever shifting scales?

The surprises will keep coming: moments of challenge, of difficulty, of unease. There will be little moments with complete strangers and there will be big moments with significant others. Last week, for example, when my own sister threw me a curve I never saw coming. My own sister – one of the few people I thought could never again surprise me – said things I could not have imagined her saying in a million years … and the smoke started rising again. I guess that muscle still needs work; I haven't yet learned to *live* that old Boy Scouts motto.

The future will continue to bring new pitches, new situations I can hardly envision today. The one thing that will not change will be the person in the batter's box: I will be in tomorrow's game, just as I was in today's, digging my cleats into the dirt, adjusting my stance, gripping the bat. I am the one who will decide how to respond to whatever comes. There can never be any autopilot for this game; the price of success, of growth, is eternal vigilance. The calculus of life is always at work and I alone am the common denominator of every second, every inning. I alone must learn how to position myself in such a way that, when the ball arrives and I swing the bat, the two will meet only that one sweet spot, create that beautiful crack of sound, and enable me to reach base not just safely, but gracefully.

Six Men and Two Dogs

There is so much in a picture. It's worth *more* than a thousand words. More like *ten* thousand. But let me make a start. The six of us are standing behind the Noon Mark Diner in Keene Valley, New York. One of the waitresses took the picture for us. We don't look like we've been camping in the Adirondacks; we look too clean. Probably we just got back from a swim in one of the hundreds of pristine, river-fed pools swirling around up there. I remember this was just after we'd finished eating. Nothing like a good meal after some hiking and swimming. Eight lives are represented by this picture. Three dads and three sons. The three sons all graduated from a place called Great Neck South High School. I was fortunate to work there for 21 years.

The guy on the left, Josh, graduated in 2000. He was in my creative writing class and, every time he handed in a paper, he surprised me by revealing yet another part of his unusual, wonderful personality. What really made me sit up and take notice was when I learned that his ballroom dancing partner was eighty-six years old. The guy next to him is Doug. He graduated in 2012 along with his buddy, David. Doug was pretty quiet in class. He sat in the back and I really didn't get to know him very well until David brought him along on one of our camping trips. Every minute of that trip brought us closer together, but when he did a handstand on the smooth stone of the gorge, then lowered his nose to within an inch of the stone and proceeded to do several beautifully balanced push-ups, I was hooked. The guy next to him is Paolo. He just graduated last year, 2020. I never met a kid his age so hungry for knowledge. And not just book knowledge. This kid already knows a lot about how to live a wholesome, loving life, and yet he's always eager to learn more, always practicing the humility that eventually brings wisdom.

Next are the three amigos, the three dads: Paul (Paolo's dad), me (neither of my two sons, Jacob and Adam, was available for this trip) and Mitch (Doug's dad). The dog on the left is Woody, Paolo's dog. The one on the right is Snickers, mine. We covered a lot of ground together, the eight of us. We spent some very beautiful hours together. We all look pretty happy, do we not? We had a blast together. The environment and the company could not have been better. But, for me, there is an additional level of pleasure. I'm not sure I can put it into words, but I'll try:

I taught English for 32 years, 11 in Brooklyn, twenty-one in Great Neck. In all those years, there were many kids I connected with, but the social boundaries and anxieties that have evolved over the decades usually prevent a teacher and a student from getting very close. The memory of all those famous cases of deviance and abuse is usually too strong to allow the natural flow of love in a classroom. When I look at this picture, besides all the great memories of backyard barbeques, visits to grandpa's house, and wonderful camping trips, I get an additional measure of joy from the consciousness that we have beaten the odds. The six of us have managed to break free of the usual constraints between teacher and student. Our love was stronger than our fear… and we became the best of friends.

My Father's Voice

Around eleven years ago, when I first started saying kaddish for my father using his own tefillin, an old shule friend of his noticed that the head part didn't quite fit; the leather was too loose, and he adjusted it for me right there in the sanctuary. But it wasn't only the size of my dad's head that was bigger than mine; it was the size of his brain too. My father was the smartest one in the room just about every time. On the off-occasion when he wasn't, he was the first one to stand, to show respect, when a surgeon or a scholar or a rabbi walked in. If he was mind, body and spirit, as we all are, then I guess this was the spirit or heart part of him. I like to think of myself as taking after him in some essential ways. I know it's a stretch for me to do this, that I'm flattering myself, but I like to do it anyway.

I published my first and only book, *A Little Consideration*, in 2011, just a year after dad died. I wish he had lived to see the book in print; he would have loved it. I can picture him carrying a few copies in his car so he could show it off and give it as a gift to relatives and friends. I'm now working on my second book, and this is its thirty-sixth story. It is entirely fitting that this writing – so much about him – should be the thirty-sixth. In Hebrew, the letter *lamed* equals thirty and the letter *vov* equals six. There is a legend in Judaism associated with that number known as "The Lamed Vov," "The Thirty-Six." It is written that, at every moment on this earth, there are thirty-six righteous individuals without whom the world would cease to exist. Part of the beauty of the legend is that we never know who these people are while they're alive; oftentimes, we later discover they were quiet, nondescript individuals. One of them could be the old lady who goes around town collecting bottles from people's recycling bins. Another could be the guy who camps out along the fence by the train station. Whoever and wherever they are, if just one of them were missing, even for a second, the world would immediately end; their goodness somehow counterbalances all the bad. When one of them dies, another is born. In this way, their number is maintained, and the world goes on.

My father had an amazing voice, both talking and singing … but especially singing. All three of us, his sons, have his speaking voice; but nobody can touch him in singing. Still, when I chant the old Chassidic melodies he taught me so well, I hear a little bit of him in me; he is alive again. There's nothing like music to stimulate memory … except maybe smell. Certain smells also whisk me back: a roasted chicken on *Shabbis*, a well-done matzoh-brei on *Pesach*. The nose and the ear are bridges to our past. To find anything that surpasses these, one must turn to fiction. In the *Harry Potter* books, the Pensieve is an external receptacle for storing memories: you pour your memories into it, and then, as though they were movies, anyone can watch them, at any time. But since I live in the real world and have no Pensieve here, I will continue to rely on music and smell to deepen my memory, to retrieve my yesterdays. I will continue to listen for my father's voice in mine, to align myself, as much as possible, with harmony, with heart, with spirit.

A couple days ago, I went to a local gas station to have a headlight replaced. I had an eight o'clock appointment, pulled up at ten-to-eight, and was about to take out something to read when one of the mechanics came over and asked, "What's up?" I told him about the headlight, but that I was in no hurry and could wait. He told me to open up the hood, took out the old bulb and went into the office to get a new one. When he got back, he was having trouble getting the new one in, so he decided to go back into the office to make sure the new one matched the old one. It did. Still, he couldn't get it in properly. After about ten or fifteen minutes of fiddling with it, not wanting to give up, not wanting to disappoint me, another mechanic, who had just pulled in, walked over and took a look. Apparently, he was more experienced with a Prius and got the bulb in easily. I figured the job would cost at least twenty dollars – especially since it took more time and manpower than I thought it would – and was pleasantly surprised when the first guy said, "Give me ten bucks."

I paid, got back in the car, made the right onto Monroe Boulevard, and another right onto Park. Then, something made me pull into the island parking lot there and go to the bakery. I bought a nice coffee ring for eleven bucks and drove back to the station. As I got out of the car, the original mechanic saw me and ran over, thinking something was wrong with the headlight. When I handed him the cake, I thought I saw the welling of tears beginning in his eyes. He said I made his day. I said he made mine, pressed his arm affectionately, and left.

Maybe it was my father's voice that made me pull into that parking lot and run into that bakery. He always went out of his way to show his appreciation to all kinds of people. I can't count how many times I saw him deliver a piece of home-made gefilte fish to a client or a length of fabric to a bank teller. He added a personal touch to almost everything he did, and this not only made him a lot of money; it also made him very well-liked. People saw and felt that what he was doing was more than just business; he was making a connection with them. I could not watch my father interact with so many people over so many years without having some of his magic rub off on me, without hearing his voice in almost everything I do.

Dumbledore, the most God-like person in Rowling's universe, reminds Harry that it is "not our abilities that define us; it is the choices we make." Similarly, the rabbis say God gave us free will so that we can feel the joy that comes from making good choices, from *loving* each other instead of hating each other. If we had no free will, we would just be puppets and God would just pull the strings. But that's not the way it is. We *choose* what we do. We *choose* who we become. I'm glad I chose to show that mechanic my appreciation for his work, for the time and consideration he gave me. For all I know, he may be one of the *Lamed-Vov*. For all I know, tonight, in the privacy of his humble little apartment, he may be sharing that coffee ring with God Himself.

This watercolor was done by my friend, Susan, in 1992. I was sitting at her kitchen table in Long Beach and she did it in about fifteen or twenty minutes. I would say that she was my girlfriend at the time, but that would be my own perception, not hers; she was too free to be anyone's "girlfriend." A couple months later, she went on a cross-country trip and I never saw her again. We exchanged some letters and I retained visions of us getting together one day, but that was not to be. I admired her level of freedom, but I don't think I could ever have been truly comfortable with it. I have always considered myself something of a rebel, but, compared to Susan, I am totally conventional.

Fox just off Peekamoose Road, Sundown, NY

Regina Ehrlich, my paternal grandmother, 1889-1981, with her five sons, four daughters, and their spouses

Yitzchak Mordechai Ehrlich, my paternal grandfather, 1882-1951

Anna Wallach, my maternal grandmother, 1897-1970

Manny Ehrlich, my father, 1930-2010

Joyce Ehrlich, my mother, born 1928

Manny and Joyce at the Concord Hotel, Kiamesha Lake, NY

Joyce and Manny's 50th Anniversary

Liza Ehrlich, my wife, born 1964

Ricky and Liza, Bedford Hills, NY, August 25th, 1996

Liza, taking it easy

Liza and Ricky, first picture, 1993

Liza, celebrating

Jacob Ehrlich, my son, born 1998

Adam Ehrlich, my son, born 2001

Jacob in flight, Peekskill, NY

Adam in flight, Far Rockaway, NY

Jacob, Arizona, 2018

Adam, frontside ollie

Liza, Adam, Jacob and me, The Grand Canyon, 2019

Snickers, born 2013

Josh Merlis, dear friend, in the Adirondacks

David Soffer and Doug Leff, dear friends, in the Adirondacks

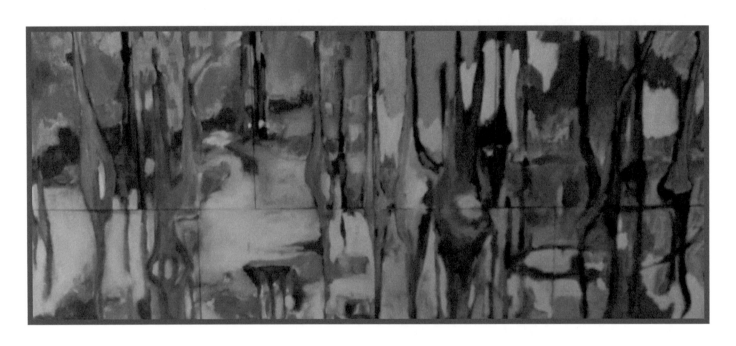

Oil on wood panels by Liza Ehrlich

Rectangle Pool, Bouquet River

Way past Guardian Rock on the Bouquet River

The Blue Hole

This painting of my paternal grandfather, Yitzchak Mordechai Ehrlich, was done by my cousin Beverly. Zada had died long before, and so Beverly used two photographs to complete the work. The first was of Zada in ordinary clothes -- no tallis or tefillin. The second was of my father wearing both tallis and tefillin. Beverly's mom, my Aunt Libby, had it hanging in her apartment down in Florida in her final years. She knew I loved it and so promised it would be mine upon her death.

This is my newest favorite picture of myself. In the past, that would mean my buck teeth were not really noticeable, or my hair was, by some fortunate accident, not looking as though I had just put my hand in an electric socket. But, with this picture, it isn't those things that make it stand out for me; it's what I see behind my smile. I see the consciousness of having driven up to the Adirondacks the day before, alone, and pitched my tent at what may be the nicest campsite I've ever had in forty years of camping. I see the consciousness of having prepared firewood that morning in such a way that a single match would ignite a conflagration that would warm me, and entertain me, for hours. I see the consciousness of having just climbed out of that magnificent body of water behind me – Chapel Pond – after a deliciously invigorating swim. I could go back days and weeks and years and recount memories of so many moments in a life that has been, for the most part, extraordinarily lucky and rich and blessed. In the single moment of my life captured in this photograph, my consciousness is filled with joy and confidence and health. I'm not feeling one iota of shame or remorse, not even for having run up to my car for the hat, just seconds before, to keep my unkempt hair from making me look like a crazy person.

I first came across the following prayer in John Irving's novel, *The Cider House Rules*. I thought it fitting that these beautiful words appear here as well, at the end of my book:

Oh Lord, support us all the day long, until the shadows lengthen and the evening comes, and the busy world is hushed, and the fever of life is over, and our work is done. Then in Thy mercy, grant us a safe lodging, and a holy rest, and peace at the last.

Printed in the United States
by Baker & Taylor Publisher Services